*Fabric Printing
and Dyeing
at Home*

Fabric Printing and Dyeing at Home

GEORGINA ALEXANDER

LONDON : G. BELL AND SONS LTD

COPYRIGHT © 1975 BY
G. BELL AND SONS LTD
Published by
G. Bell and Sons, Ltd
York House, Portugal Street
London, WC2A 2HL
All Rights Reserved

No part of this publication may be reproduced, stored in a retrieval system, or transmitted, in any form or by any means, electronic, mechanical, photocopying, recording or otherwise, without the prior permission of
G. Bell and Sons, Ltd

ISBN 0 7135 1893 6
Printed in Great Britain by
Biddles Ltd, Guildford, Surrey

Contents

	Page
Introduction	7
1 TIE AND DYE	9

    Marbling
    Rope or Twisting Method
    Binding
    Suitable threads
    Folding and Binding
    Tie and Dye with 'Found' Objects
    Tritik
    Folding and Dipping Parts Only
    Uses for Tie and Dye
    Equipment for Tie and Dye

2 WAX-RESIST BATIK   33
    The Basic Steps
    Applying the Wax
    Brushes
    Dyeing the Fabric
    Fixing the Dye
    Removing the Wax
    Equipment for Wax Batik

3 FLOUR-RESIST BATIK   43
    Dyeing Flour-Resist Batik
    Thickening Procion Dye
    Recipe for thickened Procion Dye
    Equipment for Flour-Resist Batik

4 STRING BLOCK PRINTING   52
    Equipment for String Block Printing

5 LINO PRINTING   60
    Equipment for Lino Printing

6 DYE RECIPES AND METHODS   65
    Recipe and Method for Procion 'M' and Dylon Cold, for Wax-Resist and Tie and Dye
    Alternative Recipe and Method for Procion Dyestuff
    Use of Procion for Tie and Dye Work Only

7 DESIGN   71
    The Use of Colour in Design
    General Principles
    The Use of Shape and Line
    Inspiration for Design

Suppliers in Great Britain	75
Suppliers in the U.S.A.	76
Glossary	77
Books for Further Reading	79
Weights and Measures	79
Index	80

Acknowledgements

I must thank all those who have helped me in the preparation of this book, in particular:

Ivy Haley, Lecturer in Art at Lady Spencer Churchill College of Education, for colour plates 1 to 8 and descriptive notes.

David Gully, Abingdon, Berks, for most of the black and white photographs and colour plates 9 to 13.

Liz Roberts for the diagrams.

Dennis Payne, Stockham Way, Wantage for cutting the wooden blocks for string block printing and for making the excellent metal tjanting.

Miss Hilda Jones, The Director of Studies at Denman College, Abingdon, for her kindness in allowing photographs to be taken at Denman College.

Muriel Sanderson who arranged for me to have the tie and dye work from West Africa.

Marjorie Campbell for typing and secretarial help.

Mr L. G. Cratchley of Imperial Chemical Industries Ltd for the use of their dyestuffs and ancillary chemicals.

Introduction

The aim of this book is to give a simple and yet thoroughly reliable introduction to Fabric Printing and Dyeing in the home. All methods, recipes and processes described have been used and tested in an ordinary domestic kitchen. Most of them have also been tried and practised successfully in the craft rooms of Denman College (The Women's Institutes' own college) by W.I. members, many of whom, although having had no previous experience in fabric printing, produced work of a very acceptable standard after a course of only three or four days.

Many dyes and allied chemicals are available, but the ones we have used (Procion) have been chosen for their reliability in fastness to sunlight and washing, their simplicity of method compared to other dyes, and the fact that they can be thickened with a substance, sodium alginate, (trade name Manutex R.S.) which is non-toxic and which washes out completely, leaving the dyed fabric as soft to handle as in its original state—a great improvement over some other dye thickeners.

Most people will be surprised to find that they already possess several of the skills needed for different kinds of fabric dyeing and will enjoy transferring and adapting their previous experience into this new art/craft media.

For example, Tie and Dye work using stitching known traditionally as 'tritik', is similar in preparation to the running stitches used in smocking. The hours of sewing for a large piece of work can be a very restful and enjoyable way of passing a summer's afternoon or a winter's evening. The stitching required is not nearly as exacting as embroidery or dressmaking and is therefore quite quick to execute.

Introduction

For people who want quick results with a free and more spontaneous effect, tying-up 'found' objects such as stones, corks and cotton reels, or simply folding or twisting the material before tying it tightly with string will appeal.

Those who are experienced in drawing and painting will find this a great asset in designing and producing batik work; for ease and fluency with a paint brush and an 'eye' for balance and co-ordination of line and shape are important skills which are easily transferred to this craft. An artist's experience of colour, shade and tone will also be useful, though one must bear in mind the effect that each colour will have when used over a previous one, remembering that each colour is influenced by the colour beneath it.

A more practical and craftsmanlike approach will favour cutting stencils for flour-resist batik, and designing and making string blocks for printing.

Those who enjoy visiting ethnic museums will find limitless sources of ideas and inspiration for pattern and motifs. Some of the more primitive cultures offer beautiful and strong shapes, symbols and forms which in their simplicity are easily adapted to fabric printing, and whose subtle, often earthy, natural colours suggest very attractive schemes.

The classic source of inspiration is, as always, nature.

1

Tie and Dye

Tie and Dye is exactly what it says. One simply ties up a piece of cloth and when it is dyed and untied it will be found that where the cloth was tied the tightest it will have resisted the dye and that part will remain either completely undyed or a much paler shade than the untied areas of the cloth.

Naturally, one will not be satisfied with such random results for long, and the challenge of planning and controlling the undyed areas becomes more exciting as, with experience, one realises the great possibilities that there are in this medium.

As in all methods of Fabric Printing the cloth must be thoroughly washed and prepared before use. (For notes on preparation of fabric see Chapter 2).

It is as well to begin with a few experiments on old pieces of linen or cotton sheeting or similar material. The methods are best shown by the illustrations but the basic rules are quite simple:

1 Always tie everything very, very tightly. When a piece has been bound with string it should feel very hard, without the slightest 'give' or slackness.

2 Arrange folds and gathers as evenly as possible; experience is the best teacher of this rule.

3 Always use a good large knot to start any stitching, finishing off firmly with either a knot or by tying two different ends together.

4 When planning a largish piece of work with stitching always put all the stitches in before drawing any of them up. Even if some of the work is to be dyed in later stages it must all be stitched to start with, because once one begins to gather up the work it will obviously become

distorted from its original flat shape and then it is difficult to be accurate in adding further stitching.

Some simple and effective methods for beginning tie and dye:

MARBLING

Cloth dyed by this method makes an attractive background to further, more controlled, pieces of work, either in tie and dye or batik. It can also be used as a background for creative embroidery or collage or for string block printing. Marbling is the easiest method in tie and dye and although the results are not always predictable to the last degree they are often surprisingly exciting.

Take a piece of well-washed cotton cloth of any convenient size and shape; 18" square would be ideal. Screw the cloth up into a tight ball and tie it round with string or thread until it is very tight and hard (see Figure 1).

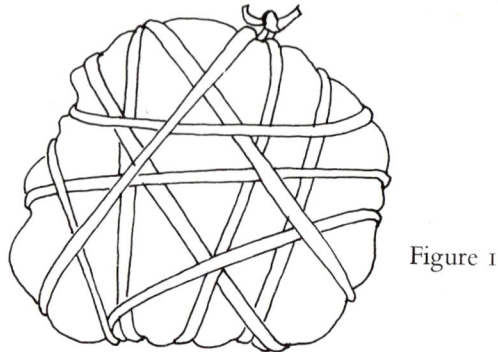

Figure 1

Fasten off the string and dye the cloth. For these first experiments it would be as well to use Dylon Cold or Dylon Multipurpose dyes. (Refer to Chapter 6 for methods and recipes.)

When the first piece of marbling is untied, you will be able to learn a good deal about the craft of tie and dye. Where the cloth was most deeply pressed into the centre of the ball it will remain white. The parts nearer to the outside will have taken some colour and the very outermost layers will be most strongly coloured. Where the string was most tightly drawn in, white lines should be left. If there is not much white left at all this is either because the cloth was in the dye too long, or, and this is most likely, because the string or thread was not pulled tightly enough. The cloth may be rearranged and retied and either dyed again the same colour or a second colour may be used. A better resist effect is obtained with Dylon dyes if the cloth is wetted in clean water and squeezed out before being entered into the dye.

Tie and Dye

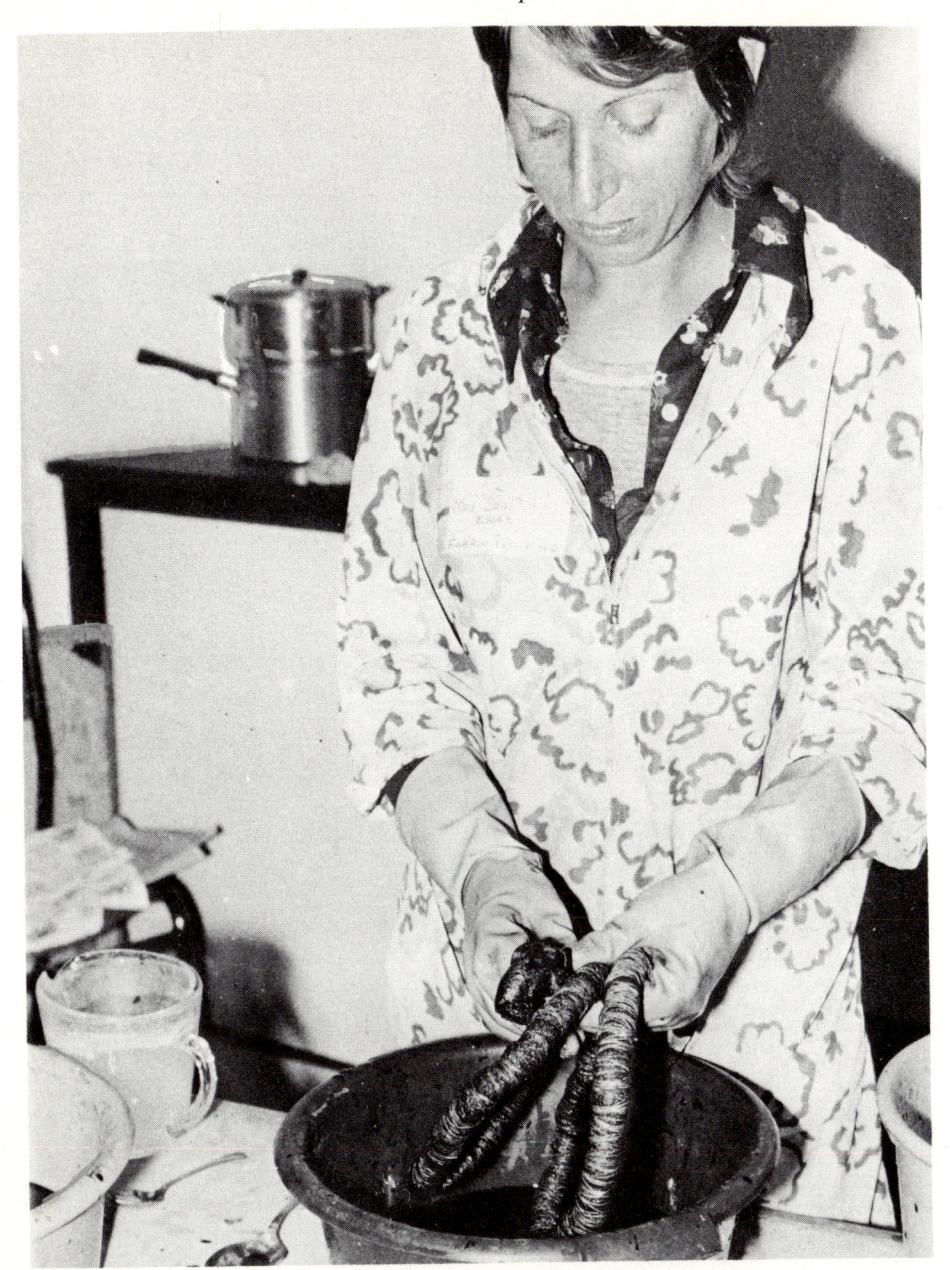

Figure 2. Mrs. Soulsby, Women's Institute member and student at Denman College Fabric Printing Course, immersing a large piece of tie-dye work into the dye-bath. The cloth has been bound very tightly with string.

Fabric Printing and Dyeing at Home

ROPE OR TWISTING METHOD

This still gives a 'background' textured pattern but of rather more controlled effect than with marbling. The coloured and contrasting areas will be more evenly distributed over the cloth. Also it is possible to dye much larger pieces by this method and it is ideal for long lengths of cloth.

Keep the right sides of the cloth outwards and gather it in the hand, keeping the folds distributed as evenly as possible. The cloth may then be tied in different ways as shown in Figures 3–6. After dyeing, the cloth may be untied and rearranged and re-tied and dyed again—the same or a different

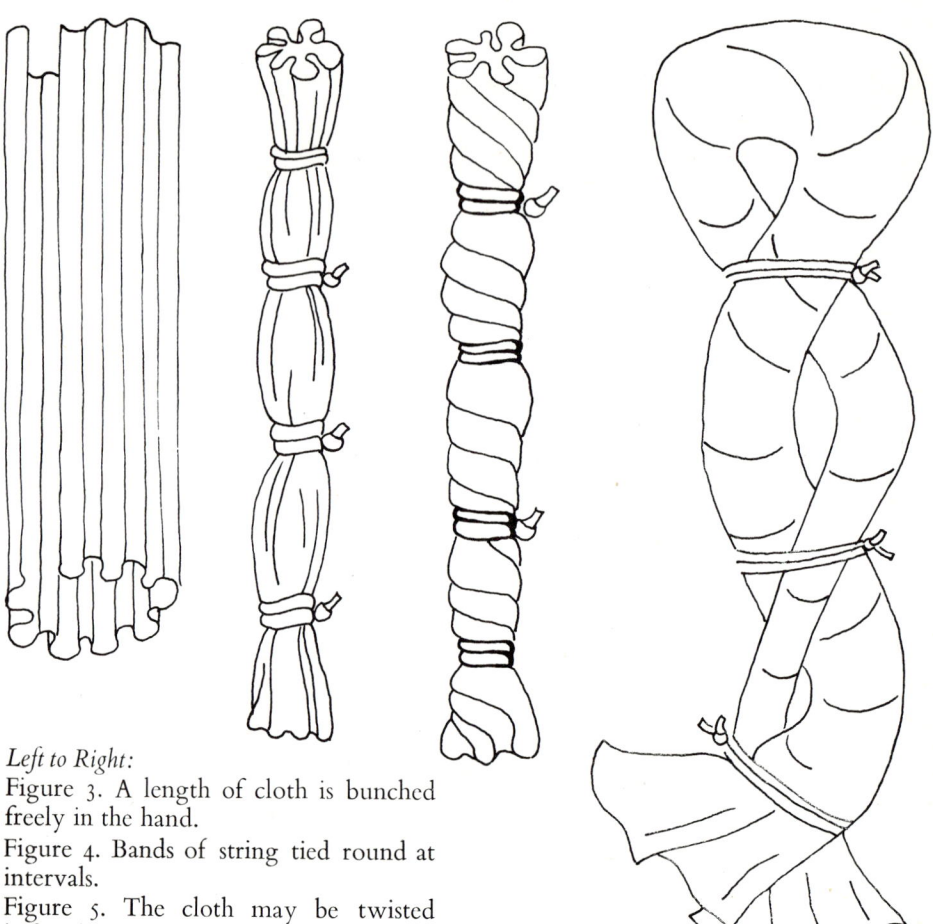

Left to Right:
Figure 3. A length of cloth is bunched freely in the hand.
Figure 4. Bands of string tied round at intervals.
Figure 5. The cloth may be twisted before being tied.
Figure 6. Twisted into a skein and bound with string.

Tie and Dye

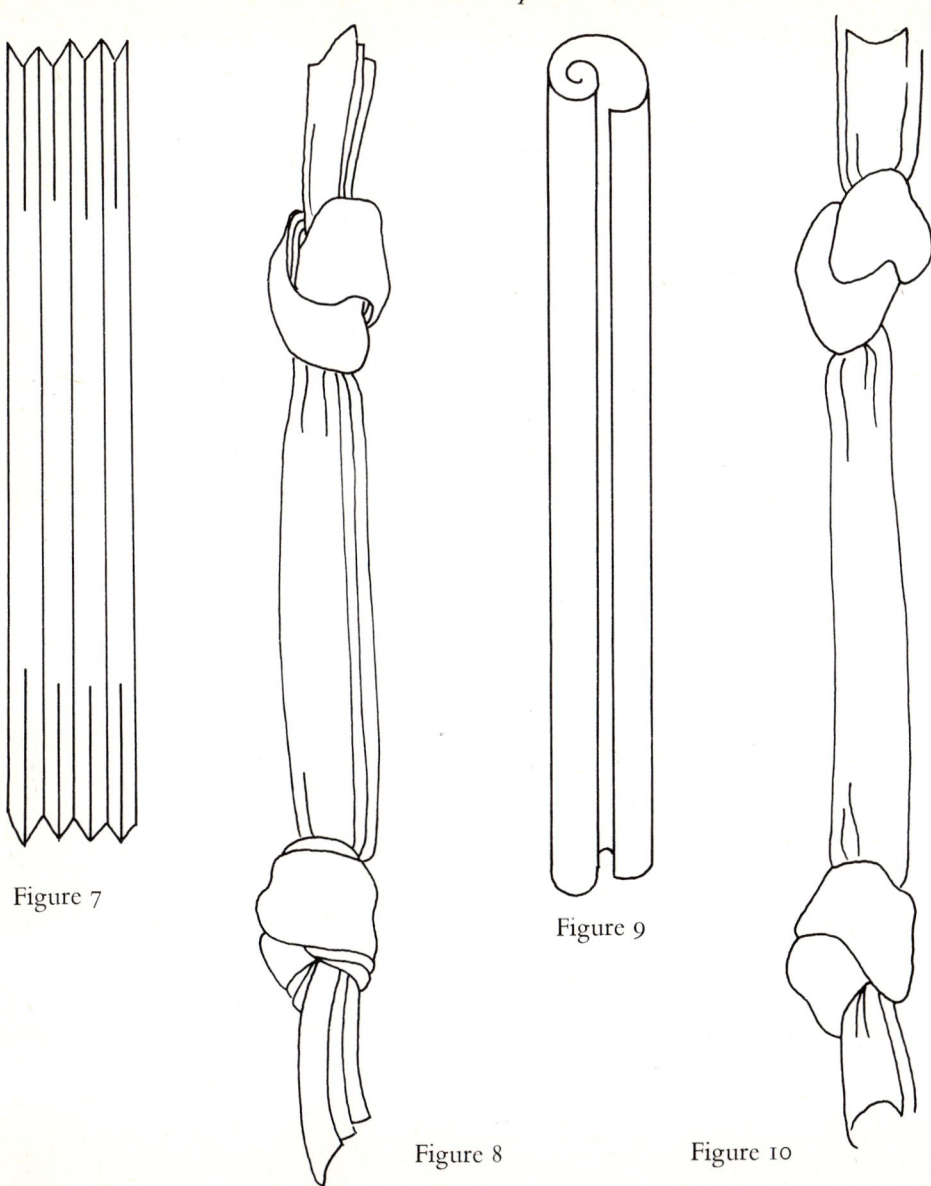

Figure 7

Figure 8

Figure 9

Figure 10

colour. Figure 7 shows the cloth ironed into zigzag or concertina pleats and then two (or more) knots are tied in it. In Figure 10 the cloth has been rolled up and then knots tied in it. This last method gives a very attractive scroll-like effect but it is only seen at its best on thin material as the dye does not penetrate so evenly on thick material. Knots may also be

13

Fabric Printing and Dyeing at Home

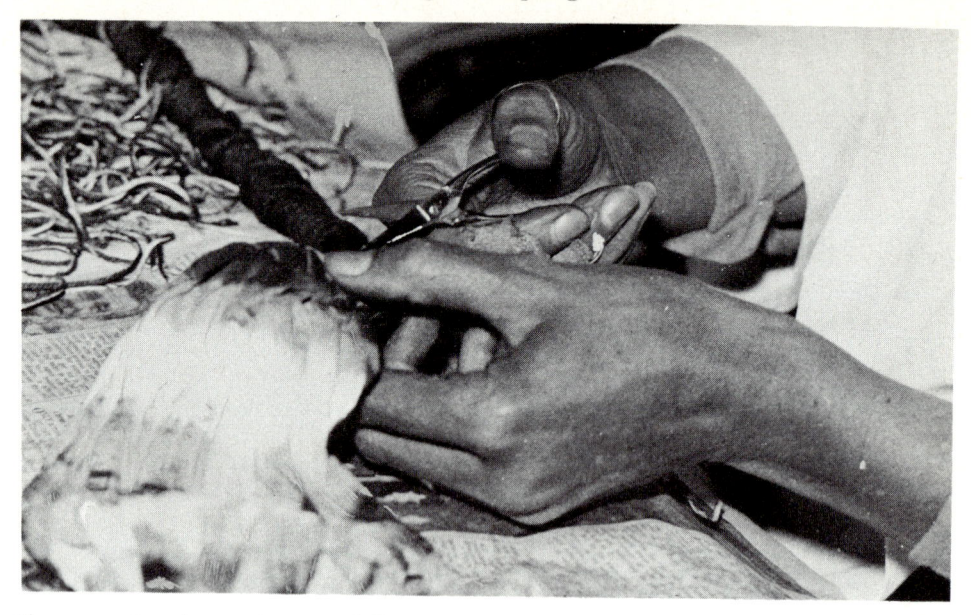

Figure 11. Another student carefully undoing the string after her work has been dyed. Great care must be taken not to cut the cloth with the scissors. The dyed string can be re-used for tie-dyeing or it can be used in collage work when it will give very attractive results.

tied in corners of rectangular pieces of cloth, and if they are pulled up quite tightly an attractive fan-like resist pattern will result. Again the most suitable cloth for knotting is a very fine one such as muslin or lawn or silk. The knotting technique will not be effective with coarse weave or thick, heavy cloths.

BINDING

This is another simple and effective way of treating fabric to produce an infinitely variable number of 'resist' patterns. The essential secrets of success are to arrange the folds or pleats in the cloth evenly, to allow even penetration of the dye and to pull the binding thread or string as tightly as possible. Of course it is equally important to ensure that the ends of the thread are securely fastened so that it cannot possibly work loose in the dye bath.

Some suitable threads for binding

Sewing cotton or sylko use double, linen thread, carpet thread, crochet cotton of various thicknesses, string of any thickness; whichever is chosen

Tie and Dye

it must be strong enough to stand being pulled very tight. Waxed string may be used, also rubber bands. Certain kinds of nylon or other synthetic threads and strings are not suitable as they have too much elasticity and can never be made taut.

When using the binding technique one may cause a blister on the finger; indeed this is a sign that the binding is being put on tightly enough. However, if the string is wound two or three times round a pencil or similar object it is possible to pull it up without causing blisters. (See Figure 12).

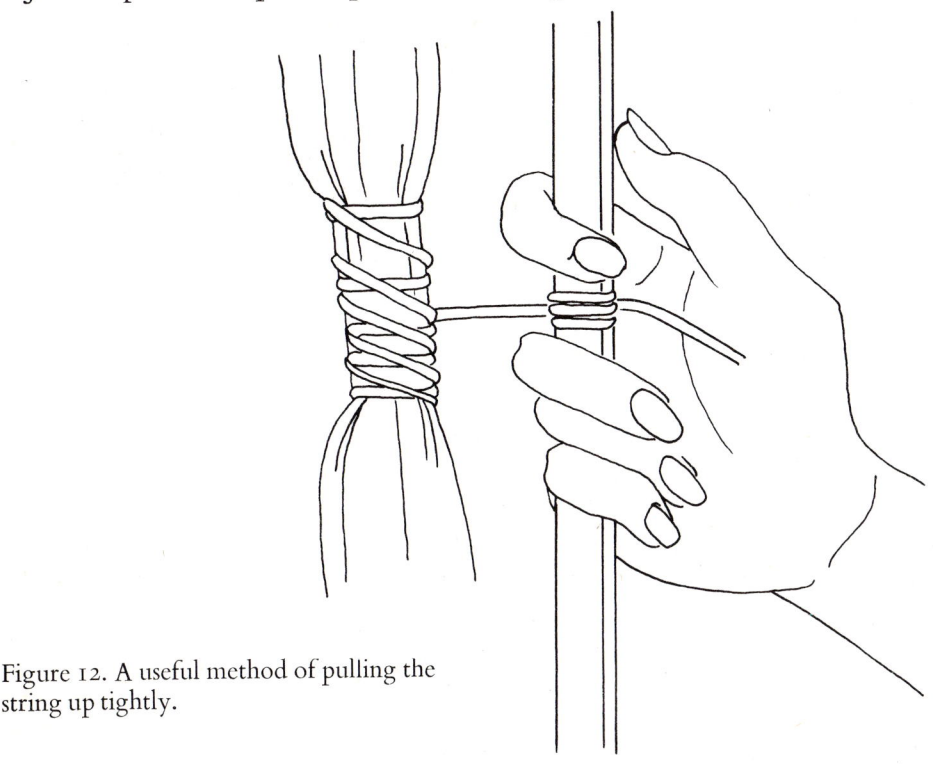

Figure 12. A useful method of pulling the string up tightly.

Figures 7–10 show some uses of binding and Figures 13–16 show further variations. Once one has gained some working knowledge of this method other possibilities will suggest themselves.

FOLDING AND BINDING

All kinds of folding and binding may be combined. Figures 17–20 show a design which is produced by folding, stitching and binding. Figures 21–23 show different ways of folding. Diagonal folding can give unexpectedly

Figure 13

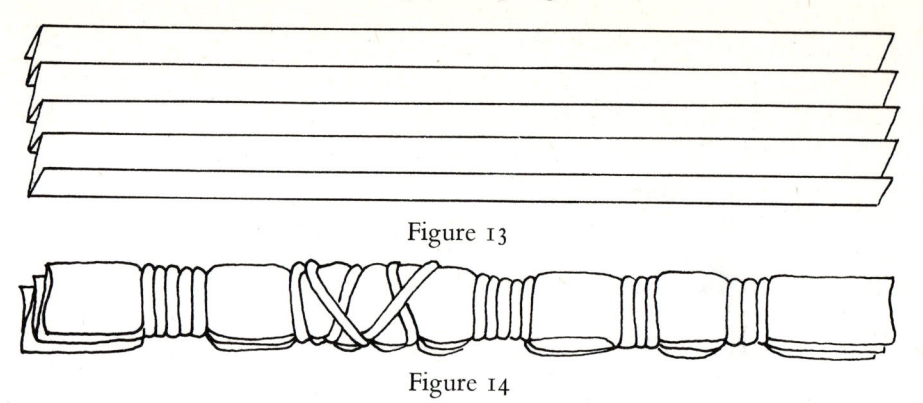

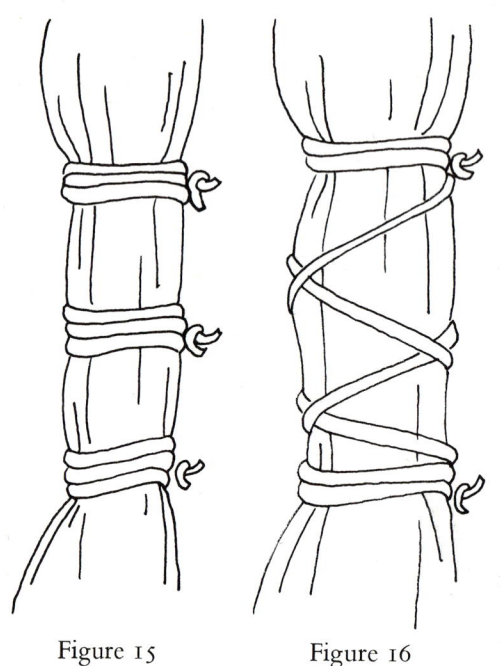

Figure 14

Figure 15   Figure 16

> *Opposite page:*
> Figures 17-20. A square of cloth is folded into four and then folded diagonally. Rows of stitches are put in through all layers of cloth. Next, the stitches are drawn up, the ends tied, and string is bound tightly in criss-cross fashion round the apex point. The other two points have two bindings of string on each and further string is tied round the triangle shape at the base. The cloth is dyed a dark olive-green, which makes a good contrast with the white resist pattern.

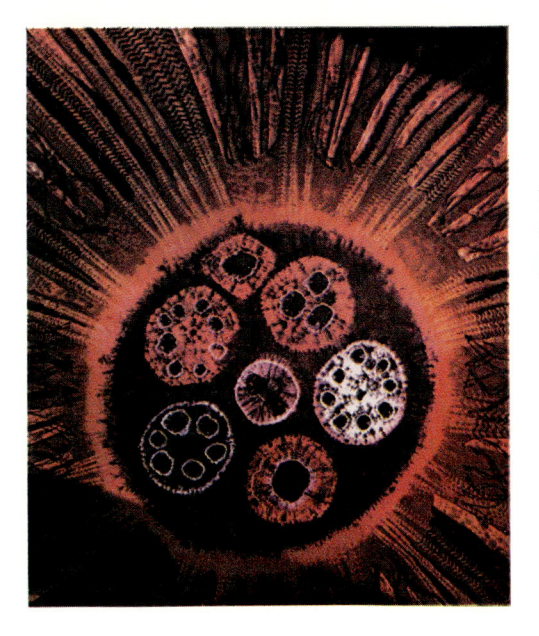

PLATE 1 A large piece of work, using Cold Water dyes for the vibrant pink and hot Direct dyes for the purples. (Designed by Ivy Haley)

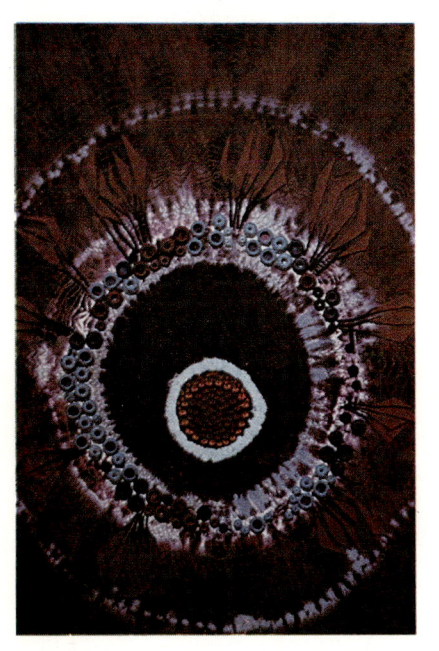

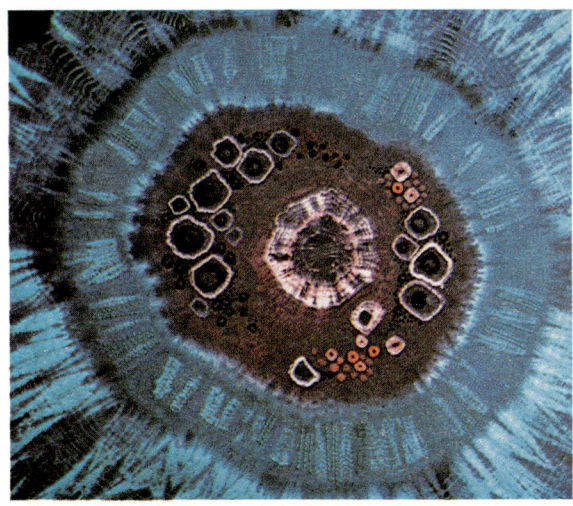

PLATE 2 Work divided into concentric circles by means of lines of stitching. (Designed by Ivy Haley)

PLATE 3 Five dyes were used for this piece of work and dip dyeing produced clear colours requiring less protective binding. (Designed by Ivy Haley)

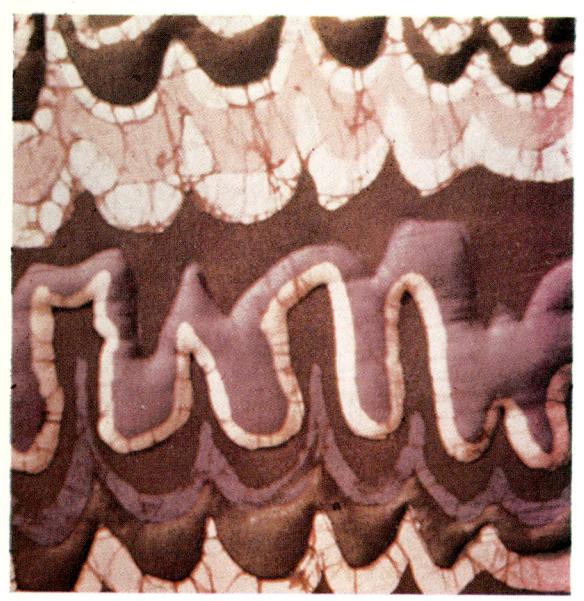

PLATE 4 Detail from a piece of batik work based on studies of a shell. It was dyed in three colours and some of the bands were then padded. (Designed and worked by Mary Jones)

PLATE 5 Detail of a larger design showing pattern obtained with simple open binding. (Designed by Ivy Haley) ▶

PLATE 6 Simple circle binding in three colours. The yellow and orange were dip dyed in order to obtain the clear colours in their own right. (Designed by Ivy Haley)

Tie and Dye

Figure 17

Figure 18

Figure 20

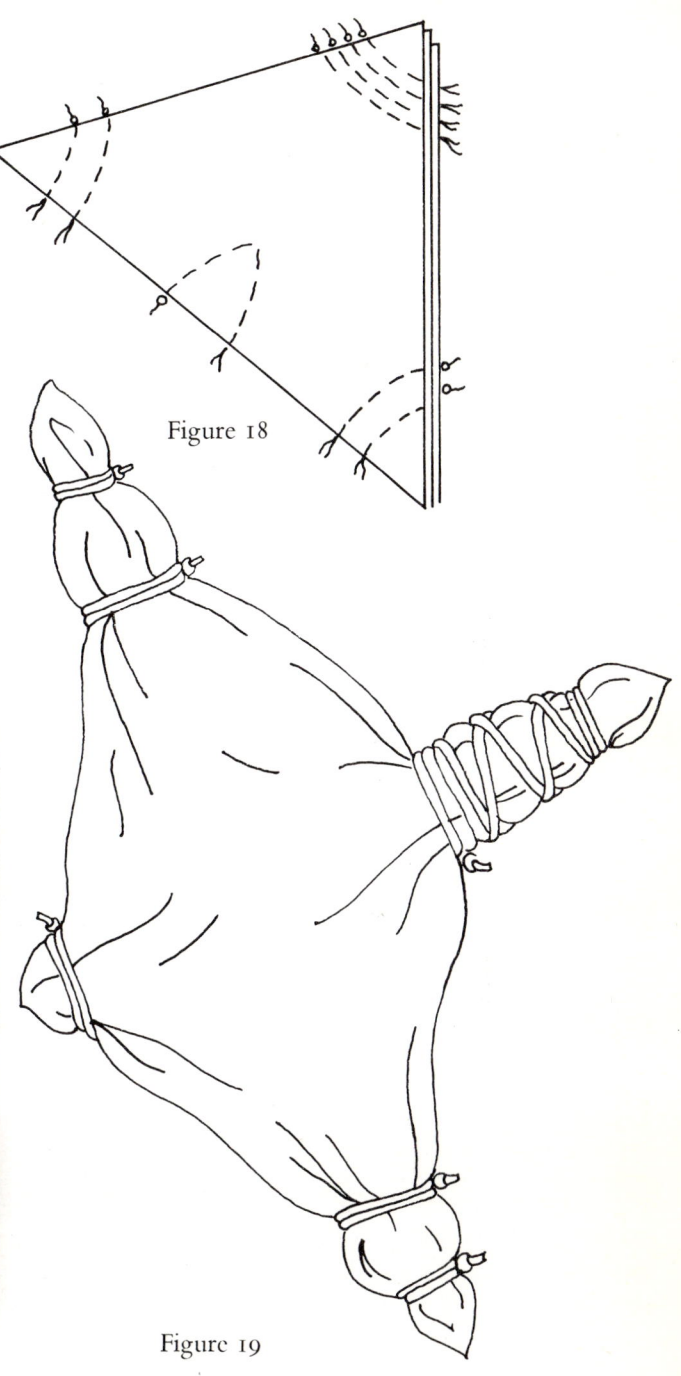

Figure 19

17

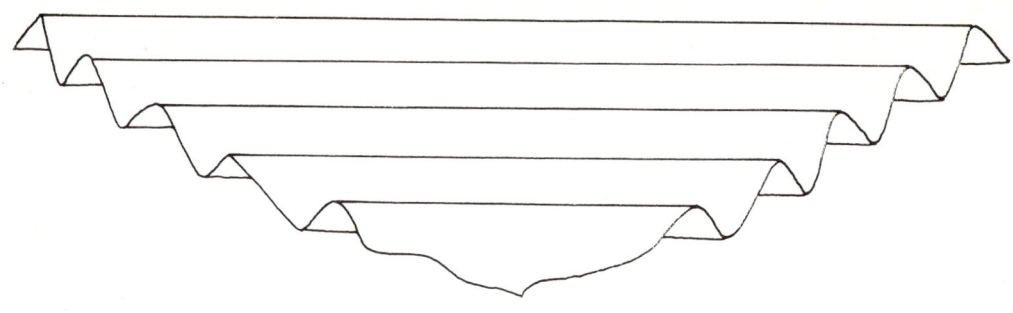

Figure 21. A rectangular piece of white cotton cloth is pleated diagonally in concertina fashion, using an electric iron to press the pleats and pins to hold them in place.

Figure 22. Nine or ten twists of string are then very tightly bound at intervals round the cloth. The pins are removed as the string is tied.

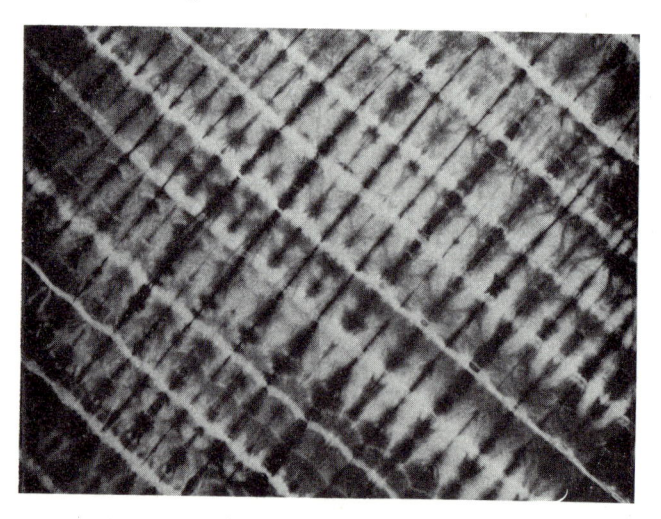

Figure 23. The cloth is dyed a dark charcoal grey. The photo shows the result. This is a simple and effective method of producing an attractive design.

interesting results. Figures 24–26 show one variation of folding the cloth on the cross:

Fold and iron the cloth into concertina pleats.

Fold the corner at an angle of 45 degrees, bringing the short edge up to the long folded edge.

Repeat this along the whole length of the cloth, ironing and pinning the folds in place.

When this folded cloth is bound tightly at intervals and dyed, an attractive zigzag or chevron pattern will result.

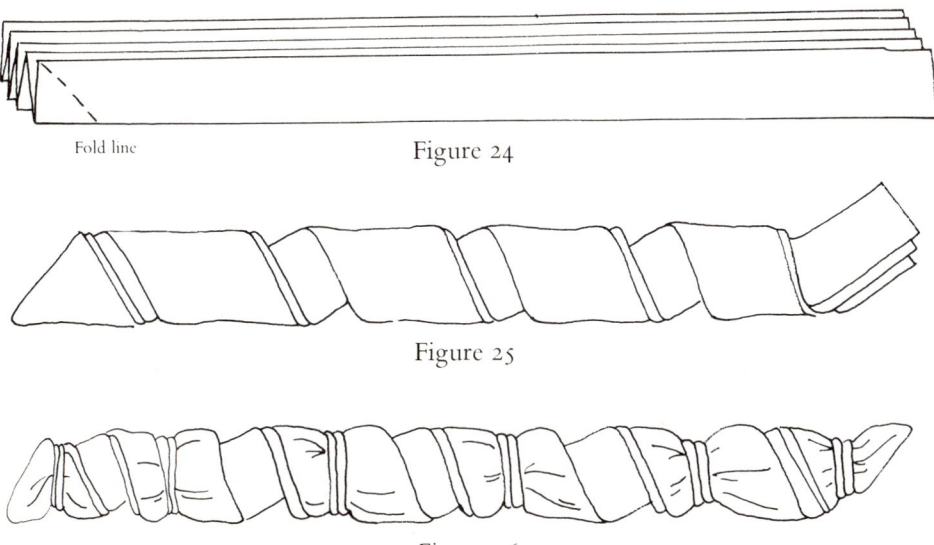

Fold line   Figure 24

Figure 25

Figure 26

The folds may be rearranged and retied and dyed again in another colour, which will give a total of three shades with an overlapping zigzag design. Figures 27-28 show yet another alternative.

Tie and dye with 'found' objects

It is traditional in West Africa to tie up seeds and stones of various sizes to produce circles both large and small. This method is readily adaptable to our use. Small stones or marbles may be tied up, also buttons of all types. (See Figure 33). Pieces of match-stick or similar square shapes will give rectangular or square patterns. Bottle corks may be bound round and tied (Figures 29–32). The amount of string and binding may be varied according to choice.

Figure 27. Fold sample vertically—then iron in concertina-type pleats.

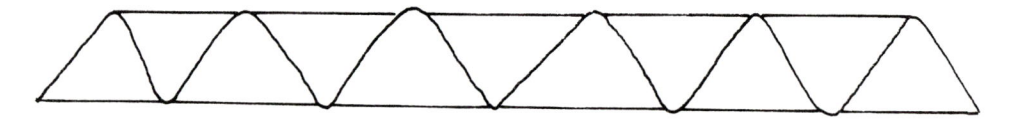

Figure 28. Finally the cloth is bound tightly with double thread or string.

When planning a large piece of work with different size circles, first mark in pencil where each object is to be tied; once the first object is tied it is difficult to see where to put in the subsequent ones unless the position is clearly marked. Figure 34 shows a plan for a square with clump tying. Five groups of small objects are tied up (Figure 35) and the square is dyed. Then further binding is put round each group (Figure 36) and the square is dyed another colour. Further tying may be added at this stage or a border colour may be added as described in Figures 46-48. This again is just an introduction to a method which offers wide scope for variation. Tiny seeds such as rice, lentils or beans may be tied, also pieces of cork, polystyrene, pieces of wood, stones, beads and cotton reels. The different shapes will produce different effects when they are tied and dyed, and the amount and position of the binding will also affect the results.

Tie and Dye

Bottle cork

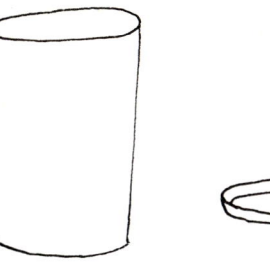

Figure 30

Buttons of various types

Figure 31

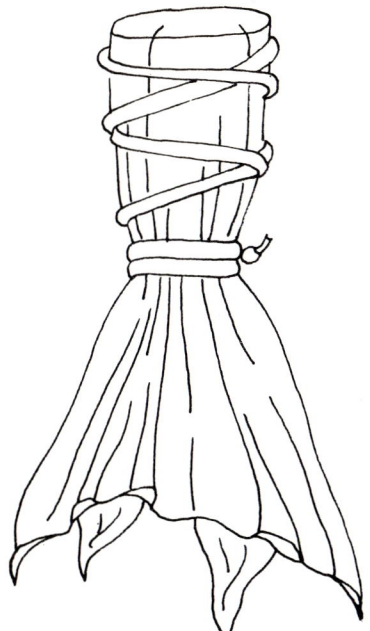

Figure 29

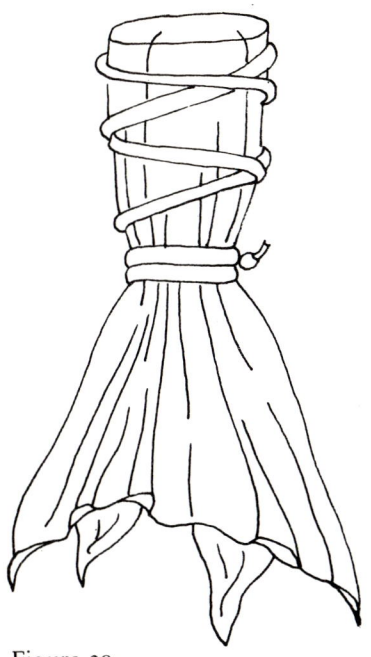

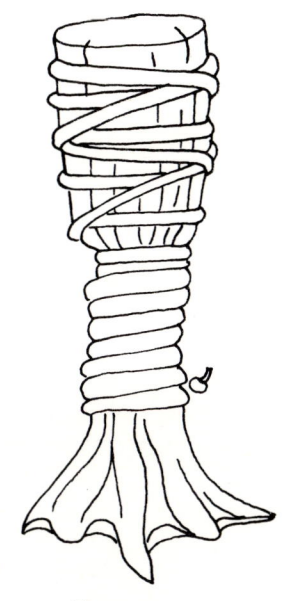

Figure 32

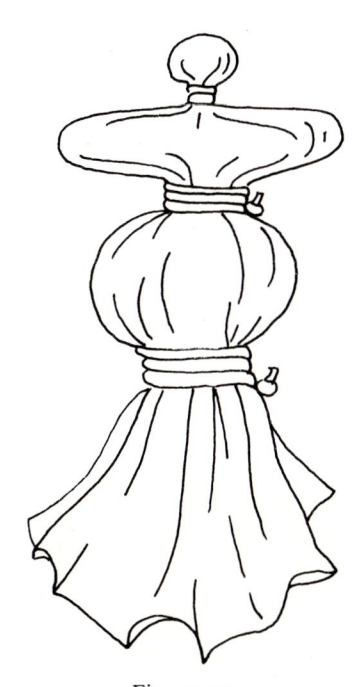

Figure 33

21

Fabric Printing and Dyeing at Home

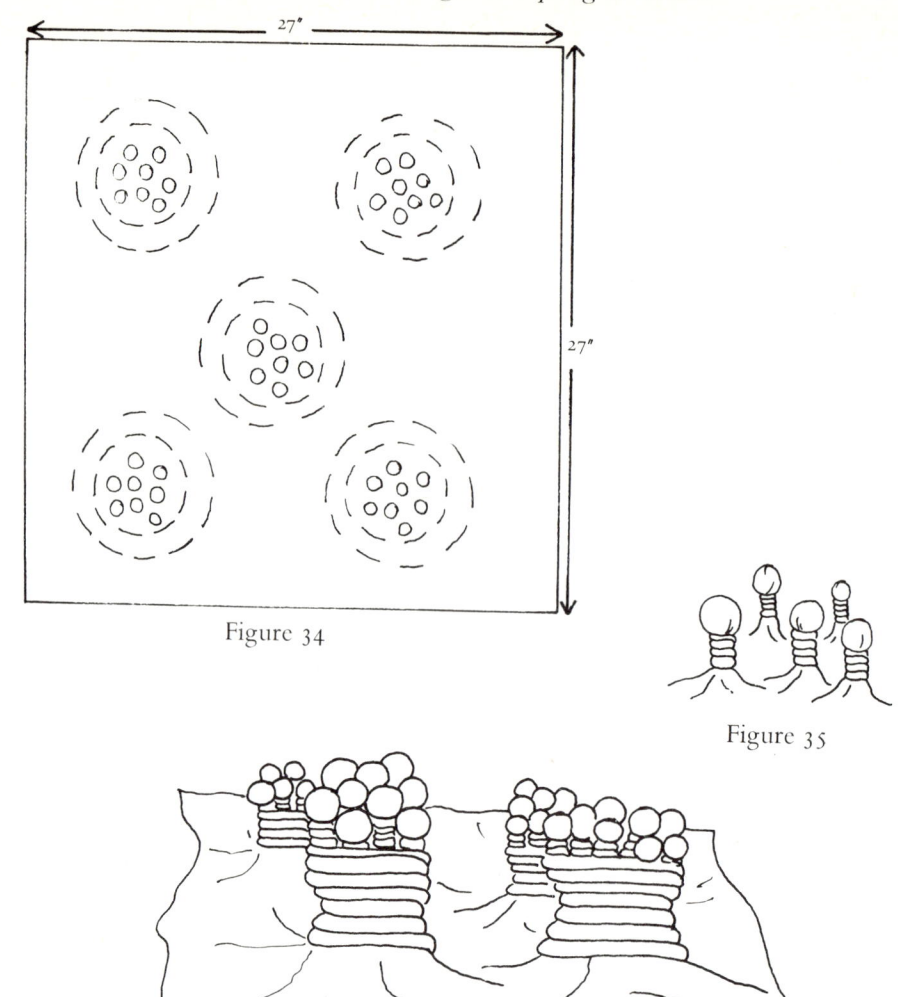

Figure 34

Figure 35

Figure 36

TRITIK

Tritik is the traditional word to describe the sewing method of tie and dye. With this method it is possible to achieve more detailed control of design and results than with any other. In fact, some people find the sewing and

22

Tie and Dye

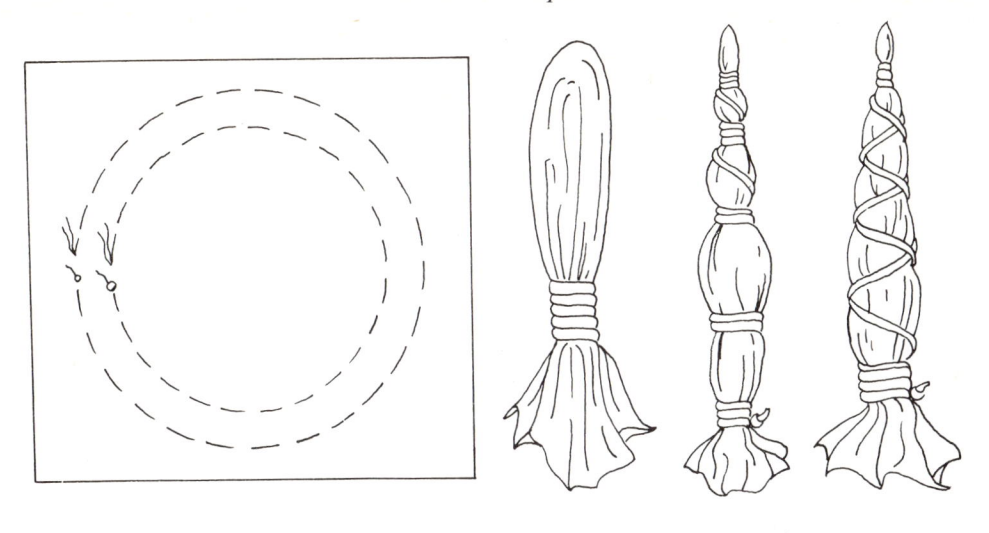

Figure 37   Figure 38   Figure 39

Figure 40. Enlarged view of Tie and Dye work from Sierra Leone.

stitching methods are far more satisfactory than any of the others because of this greater degree of control.

It is essential to have a large knot for starting any piece of sewing. Always use a strong thread or double cotton which will stand the strain of being pulled up tightly without breaking. Always measure out enough sewing thread to complete the line of sewing without having to finish off and start a new length of thread in the middle. All the threads should be put in before drawing any of them up. Then the parts which are to be left white may be drawn up and tied off. The cloth is dyed the first colour, and then the second lot of stitches may be drawn up and tied or fastened off and the second colour dyed and so on.

Figure 41 shows alternative types of running stitches. It saves time to have the cloth double or even folded into four where this is possible. One must bear in mind that the innermost folds of cloth may take up less dye, particularly if the cloth is of medium to heavy weight.

Other varieties in the work may be obtained by dipping only parts of the cloth into dye, e.g. Figures 37 and 38, a stitched circle bound.

The cloth above the string may be dipped into dye leaving the rest of the cloth in its original colour. Any number of such circles on one piece of cloth

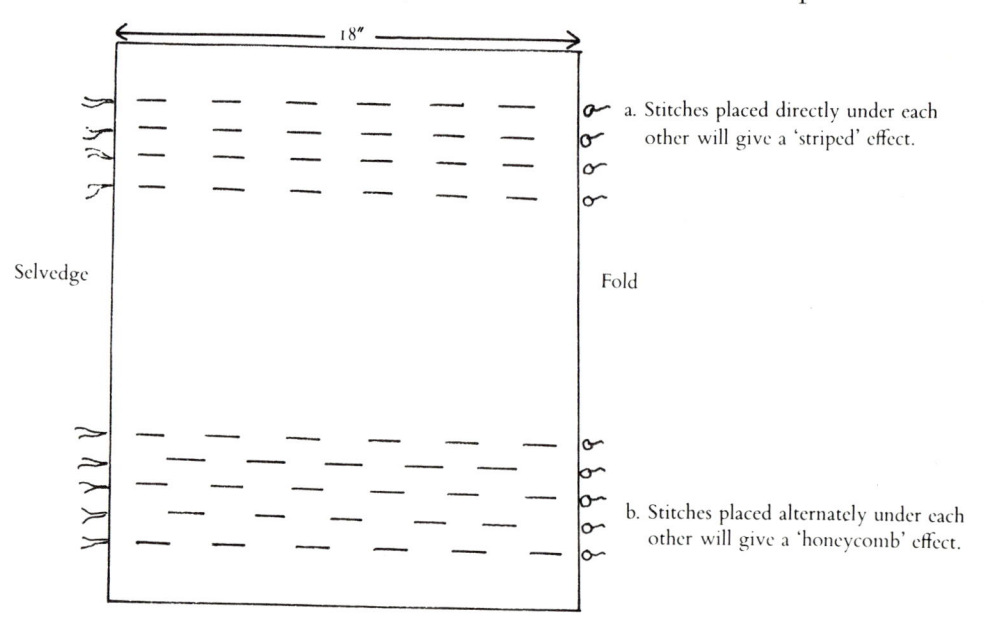

a. Stitches placed directly under each other will give a 'striped' effect.

Selvedge   Fold

b. Stitches placed alternately under each other will give a 'honeycomb' effect.

Figure 41. The stitches are approximately 1" long and 1" apart. The width between the rows may be varied from about $\frac{1}{2}$"-2 or more inches.

Tie and Dye

may be dipped. Further string (Figure 39) may be added and then the cloth dyed again; either all over, or again, just the circles may be dipped. Polythene may be wrapped and tied round some areas to reserve even larger areas of cloth.

FOLDING AND DIPPING PARTS ONLY

Figures 42 and 43 show cloth folded flat and bound; either or both ends of these 'parcels' may be dipped to give a striped effect. Further string and further dyeing may follow or the cloth may be unfolded and rearranged, retied and dyed again.

Here is another method of sewing and binding which produces a delicate 'ruched' effect. A piece of cloth is folded over and gathered in four rows through both thicknesses of cloth (see Figure 44), a piece of wooden dowel

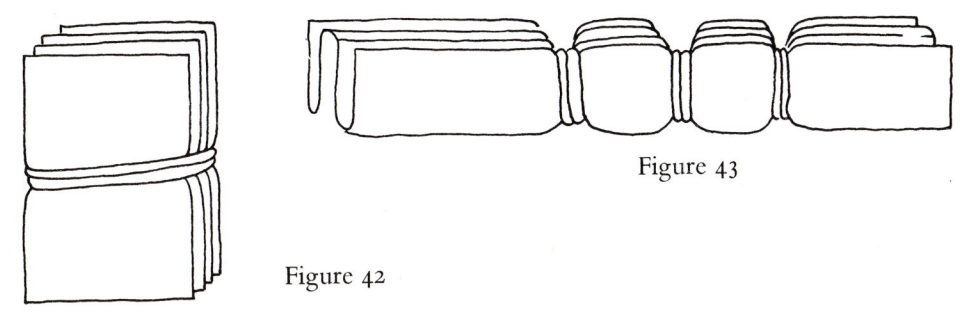

Figure 43

Figure 42

rod is put through the fold, and the gathers are drawn up as tight as possible. String is bound tightly round the wood and round the gathers (Figure 45). The cloth is then dyed with the wood still in it; further binding may be added if desired, and then further dyeing.

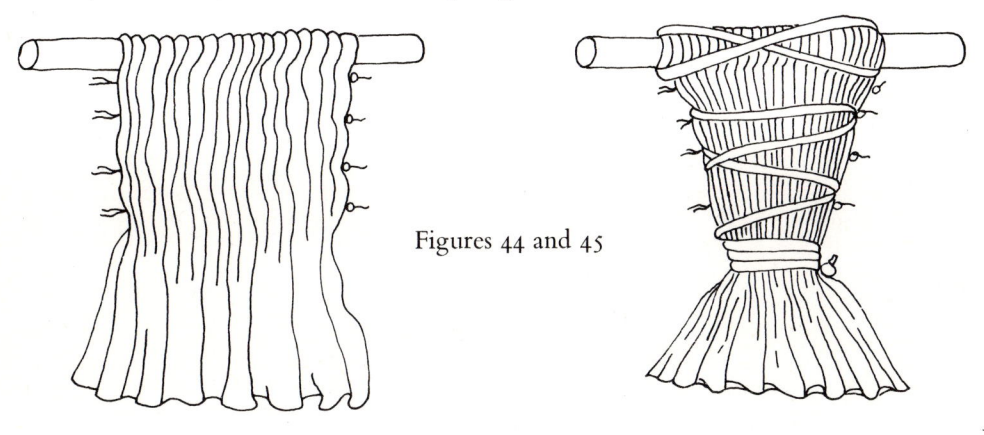

Figures 44 and 45

Fabric Printing and Dyeing at Home

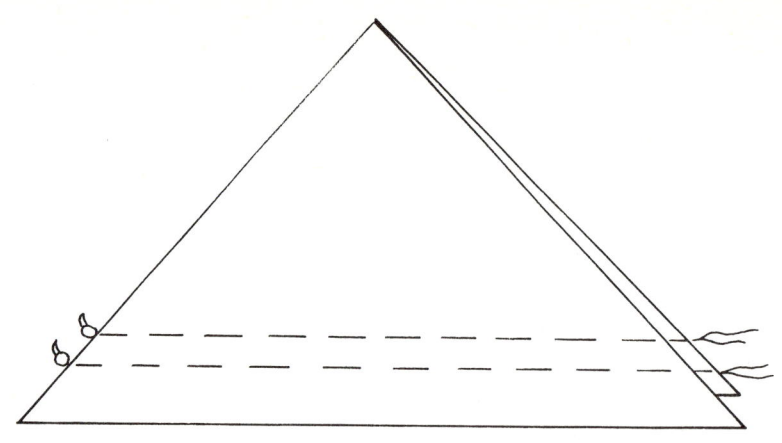

Figure 46. Preparing a square of cloth so that the edges only may be dyed.

Figures 46-48 show how a square is prepared for edge dyeing. After having patterned and dyed a square scarf or, perhaps, a tablecloth and napkins, a good finish to the design may be obtained by bordering it with a darker or contrasting colour. The square is folded in four bringing all four outer edges together (Figure 46). Two or more rows of running stitches are put in through all thicknesses of cloth. These are drawn up and fastened off firmly. To ensure a good protection for the middle of the cloth, strips of polythene may be wound round the stitched part and up over part, or all, of the centre. The free edge of the square may now be dipped into the dye.

N.B. In all mention of dyeing it is presupposed that the process of dipping in acetic acid and bicarbonate of soda will be followed when using Procion Dyes. See Chapter 6.

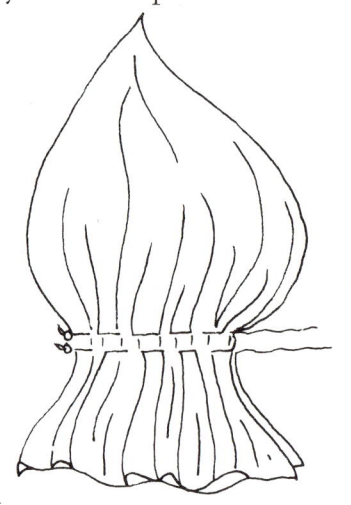

(*Left*)
Figure 47
(*Right*)
Figure 48

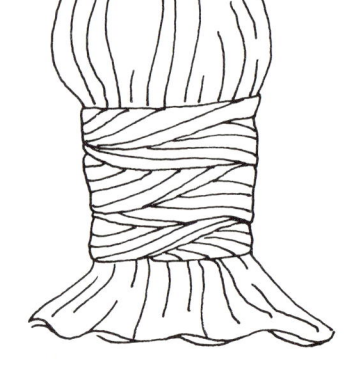

Tie and Dye

Tie and dye work can also be a basis for creative embroidery, as is illustrated by some of the colour plates. In order to keep the colours clear and bright, the colours may be dip-dyed in certain areas first, and then parts of these dipped colours may be tied or stitched and dyed, and then part or the

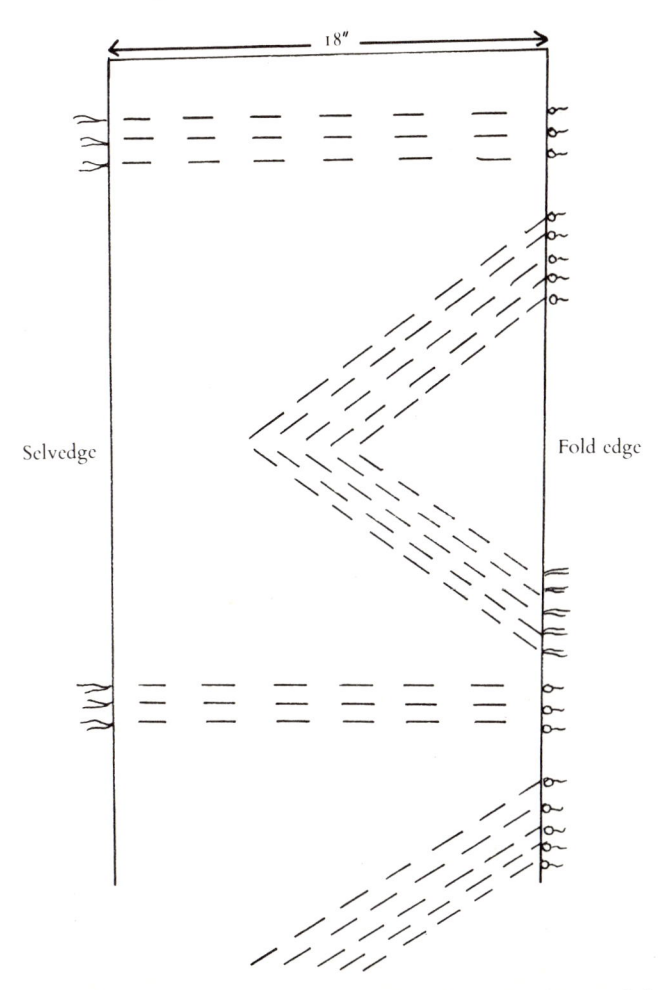

Figure 49. A simple repeat design for a length of cloth. All the stitches are put in a white cloth. METHOD: The three central rows of the triangular shape are drawn up and fastened off tightly. The cloth is then dyed a pale shade. The remainder of the triangle lines are drawn up and all those lines are tightly bound over with string and dyed again a darker colour (or a contrasting colour). Finally, the straight lines are drawn up, bound over with string and dyed the last and darkest colour.

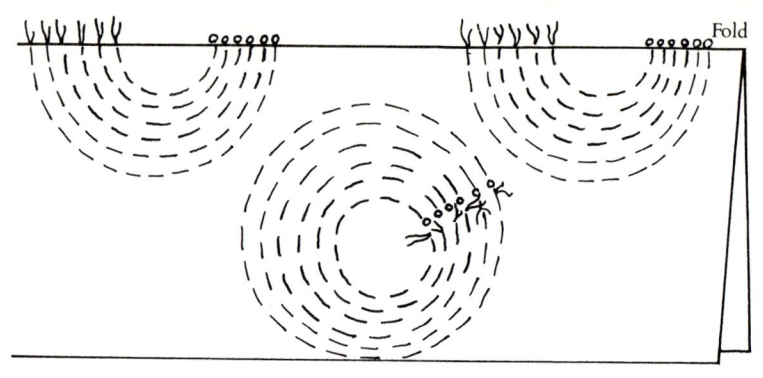

Figure 50

whole may be dyed again. The textures and shapes produced by the tie and dye may then be developed with embroidery or collage work.

Plate 1 (Colour section) shows a large piece of work, using Cold Water dyes for the vibrant pink and hot Direct dyes (e.g. Dylon Multipurpose would be suitable for home use) for the purples. The smaller circles were tied first, using variations of simple clump binding and marbling, some protecting the original white fabric and others the first pink dye. After the first dyeing, the large pink circle was stitched in order to produce a definite shape and a wide band of close binding was used to resist the purple dye. The area outside this circle was pleated and overstitched, producing a chevron pattern. To enrich this outer area, strands of hessian were couched and fly stitch was applied to emphasize the chevron pattern produced by the stitched tie and dye method.

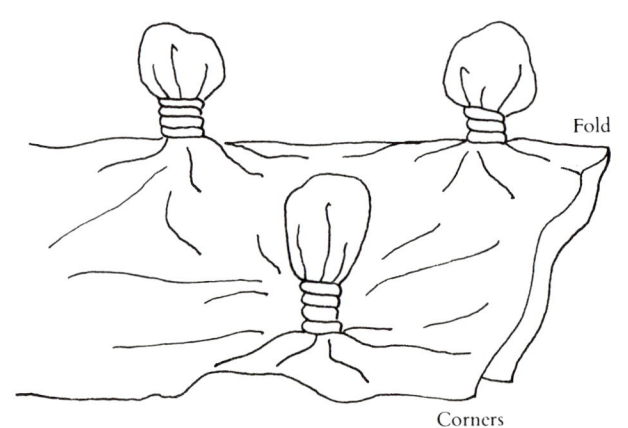

Figure 51

Tie and Dye

Figure 52. One end of a long scarf in pure silk. Both ends of the scarf have been treated in exactly the same way.
METHOD: The silk is folded in half longways. Two semi-circles are lightly drawn in pencil or tailor's chalk against the folded edge of the cloth and one full circle just below these as shown. Six rows of running stitches in double sylko are put in through both thicknesses of cloth. As with all stitch work a large knot is used to begin and the ends are left loose for the time being. Of these sets of six rows of stitches, the two centre rows are drawn up tightly; the knotted end and the loose end are tied together and double sylko (or a similar thick thread) is wound five or six times tightly over the gathers. (See Figure 51.) The scarf is then dyed a pale yellow. The two remaining pairs of rows of running stitches are drawn up tightly as before; more binding is added, completely covering all the rows of stitching, and the scarf is dyed a pinkish red. This colour—over the yellow—produces a strawberry shade. Further binding is added and the scarf dyed a dark red. The finished scarf is a dark brick red with motifs of white, yellow, pink, and a darker pink. The edges are hand rolled and hemmed.

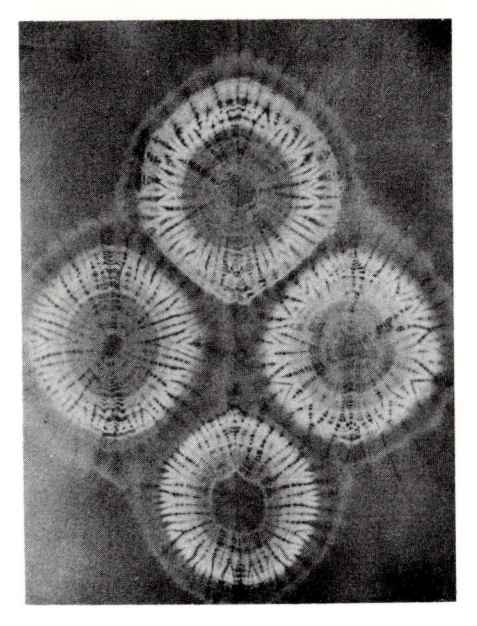

Five dyes were used for the piece of work shown in Plate 2 (Colour section) and dip dyeing produced clear colours requiring less protective binding. The central purple area was treated with varied bound circles, the outer ones having single bindings around small stones and the central, larger one being bound over a piece of cork and having a stem of criss-cross binding. This area was first dyed pink and then dyed in a plum colour. During dyeing the area outside was divided by a line of stitching and protected by a tight band of string over a strip of polythene. Next, the central area was protected and the fabric around this dyed kingfisher. A second line of stitching was then sewn and pulled up a few inches outside the first line surrounding the central area, and some of the folds produced within this band were treated with overstitching.

At this stage the band was dyed blue—the fabric on both sides having been protected. Next the kingfisher corners were bound, the blue band protected, and the whole dyed purple. Finally, stitching was added to some areas.

Plate 3 (Colour section) shows a piece of work divided into concentric

Fabric Printing and Dyeing at Home

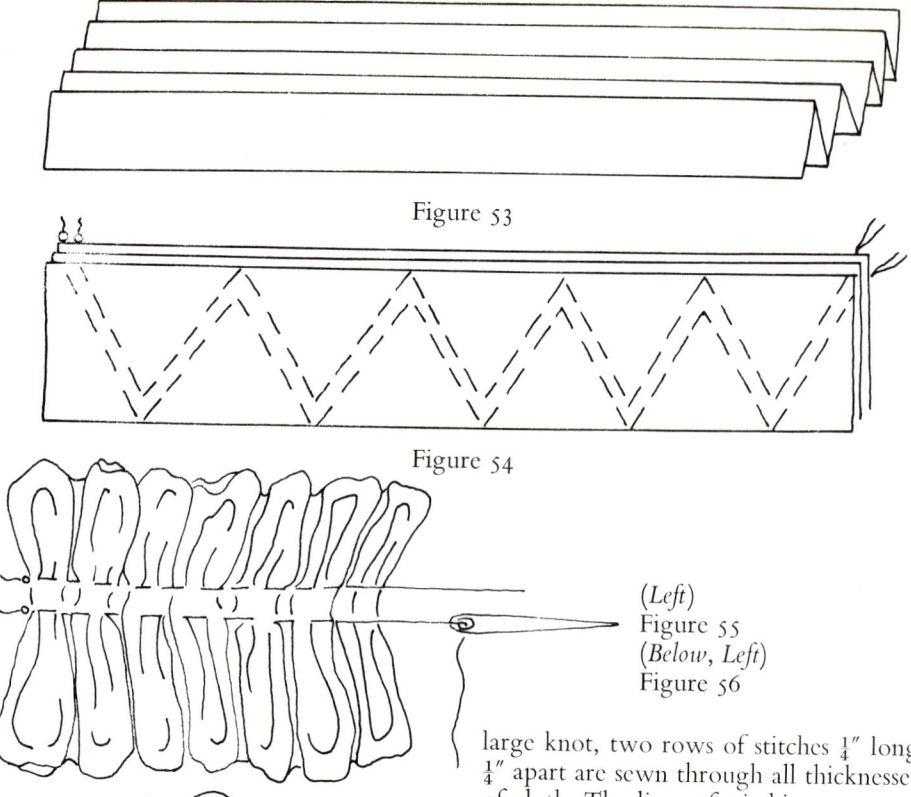

Figure 53

Figure 54

(Left)
Figure 55
(Below, Left)
Figure 56

Figures 53-57. One end of a long scarf in pure silk. This pattern continues over the whole scarf. METHOD: A length of pure silk is folded into concertina pleats and each pleat ironed into place. Using double sewing thread with a large knot, two rows of stitches $\frac{1}{4}''$ long $\frac{1}{4}''$ apart are sewn through all thicknesses of cloth. The lines of stitching must remain parallel and must not cross each other. The two rows of stitches are then pulled up tightly and tied together. Large stitches—$1''$–$1\frac{1}{2}''$ long—are sewn through all thicknesses of cloth, drawing it up as tightly as possible, at the same time keeping the work flat along the line of stitching in order that the dye can penetrate evenly. At this stage the scarf is dyed a lemon yellow and the large stitches are taken out. The folds are rearranged a little and large stitches sewn in again, this time covering even more of the cloth. The scarf is then dyed a pale turquoise blue. The result is an even and delicate pattern in white, lemon, pale turquoise blue and greenish-blue where the two dyes were together.

Tie and Dye

Figure 57

circles by means of lines of stitching. When gathered up, the smaller one was bound closely to produce a single band of colour and the next was treated with a wider band of open binding. The whole of the area within the small central circle was covered with small eyelet holes worked in fine threads of golden brown tones. The dark area surrounding this was left in its plain dyed colour but the next band already patterned by tie and dye is enriched with stitching and covered rings, producing a rich texture. Felt shapes cut to emphasize the pattern produced from the earlier tie and dye were applied on the outer band.

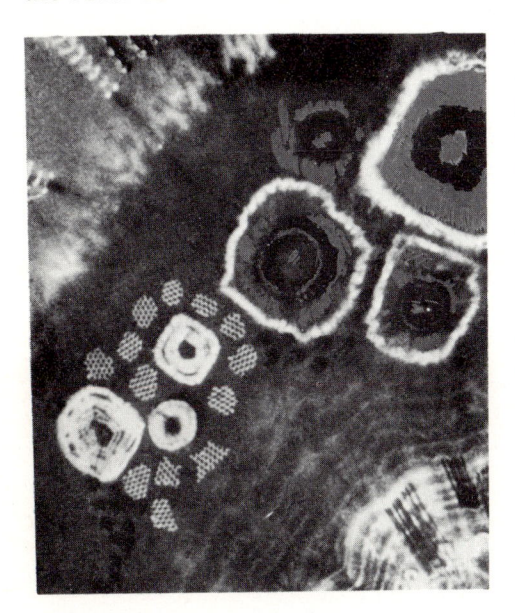

Figure 58. Part of Colour Plate 2 shown in more detail. The larger circle has had fine stitches added and a length of mohair loop couched to introduced a touch of brilliance. Some washers, rings and small cones have been covered in purple wool and attached within the smaller circles and the background enriched with stitches and small applied shapes. The blue band has had strips of net and bands of stitching applied between the tie and dye patterns.

Figure 59. Close-up of textured area on the work shown in Plate 3. The covered washers, rings, felt shapes and stitches emphasize the pattern already produced by tie dyeing.

USES FOR TIE AND DYE

Scarves (long or square) table linen, cloths, luncheon mats, serviettes or napkins, cushion covers, table centres, chair backs, borders on curtains in net or fine material; cotton for bedspreads, dress or blouse lengths, children's clothes; silk for making into lampshades, velvet or silk for evening skirts; towels and flannels and towelling for bathroom curtains. Any of these items dyed with Procion will be fast to washing and sunlight. One of the great advantages of dyeing one's own furnishings etc., is that the colours may be matched or contrasted to one's own choice. For clothing such as blouses, only part of the finished garment need be patterned, for instance, a line of tie and dye down the length of the sleeves, or a large motif on the back and front of a blouse will be very effective. The other parts of the garment may be dyed plain colour.

Equipment for Tie and Dye

String—fine or medium thickness
Sewing threads—sylko, cotton or thick crochet cotton
Needles, scissors
Objects to tie up, e.g. buttons in various sizes, beads, seeds, small stones, and corks
Chalk to mark designs
Iron and board

PLATE 7 In this panel the circles were defined by stitched lines before the binding was applied. (Designed by Ivy Haley)

PLATE 8 Batik panel showing some areas where the wax was applied by brush and others where a tjanting was used. The large areas of colour were obtained by immersing the fabric in a dye bath but some of the smaller areas of colour were painted on. (Designed and worked by Anne Young) ▶

PLATE 9 Finished scarf illustrated in the process of making in wax batik.

PLATES 10–12 Samples of tie and dye from Sierra Leone.
The panels shown in Plates 10 and 11 (*Above*) are approx. 2½ by 1½ yards.

Plate 12 (*Below*) shows a detail from a larger panel, 18 by 15 in.

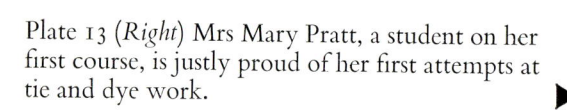

Plate 13 (*Right*) Mrs Mary Pratt, a student on her first course, is justly proud of her first attempts at tie and dye work.

2

Wax-Resist Batik

Batik, like Tie dyeing, is a 'resist' method of dyeing fabric. In this case instead of tying up the cloth to prevent the dye reaching all parts of it, it is patterned with hot liquid wax, which, once it is cool, will preserve the original colour of the cloth when it is put in the dye.

Batik is a very old craft originating in Java and practised in Eastern countries such as Malaya, Japan and India. Fragments of batik cloth were found in the tombs in the pyramids which suggests it is at least 2,000 years old. The best examples of wax batik to be seen in our museums and ethnological collections are from Java and Sumatra, where the patterns often have a traditional significance.

Batik is an attractive craft to practise at home, and one that is relatively simple to master in its basic techniques. With a little practice it is possible to produce work of a very high standard and which can be adapted to all kinds of uses.

The Basic Steps:

1. Apply the wax
2. Dye the cloth
3. Fix the dye
4. Remove the wax

If so desired, these four steps may be repeated over and over again to build up a succession of colours in an intricate design.

As with all fabric printing the material used must be thoroughly washed to remove all dressing before use.

In schools, and whenever young children are about, the wax should

Figure 60. A tin with candle wax in it is heated in a saucepan of water over an electric ring. The tjanting has just been brought out of the hot wax. When the tjanting is moved over to the cloth it should be kept level so that the wax will not drip.

be heated in a tin which is stood in a pan of boiling water. However, for adult use the wax may be heated directly over an electric hot-plate or ring. If available, a sugar-boiling thermometer can be used to test the temperature; 260°-280°F will give best results. Great care should be taken to avoid accidents with the hot wax as it is highly inflammable.

Figure 61. Here the wax is being heated directly. Great care must be taken to avoid accidents and it is not advisable to heat it in this way over a naked flame such as gas. A sugar-boiling thermometer is used to gauge the temperature: 260°F-280°F is ideal. A homemade tjap —see Figure 62—has just been dipped into the wax and given a light shake to remove excess drips.

Wax–Resist Batik

1 APPLYING THE WAX

Traditionally, in Java and Sumatra, the wax was applied with a tool called a *tjanting*, which will draw fine lines or make dots or spots, or with a *tjap*, which is a metal stamp consisting of fine strips of metal shaped into a design. This stamp is dipped into the hot wax and then banged hard onto the cloth. Figures 62-63 show a tjap made commercially by Mr. Dennis Payne; it is made of pure tin mounted on a wooden base. The circles are of $\frac{1}{2}''$ copper pipe.

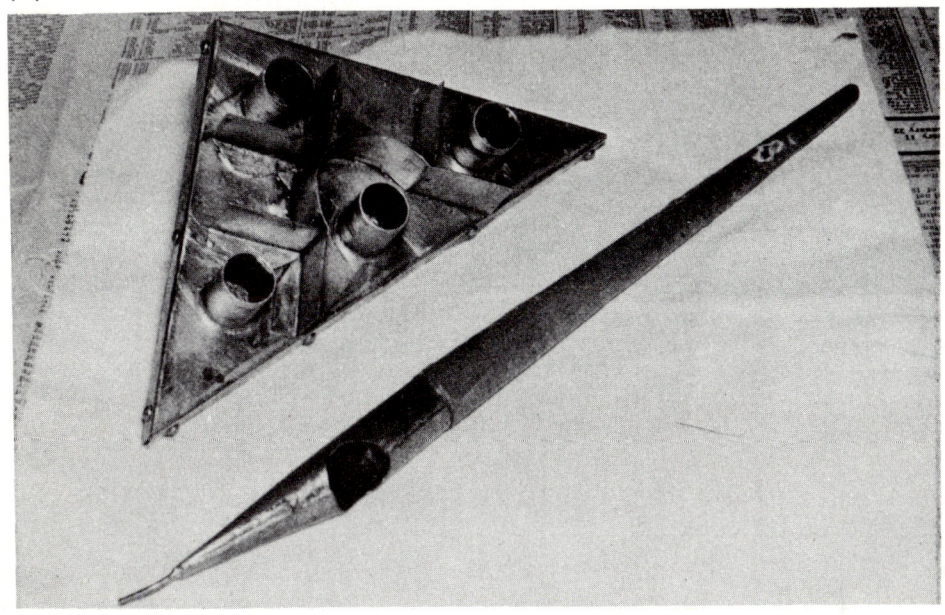

Figure 62. Tjap made of tin and copper-pipe mounted on a wooden base. The tjanting on the right is made of copper and brass on a wooden handle. A basic triangular shape was chosen for the tin and copperpipe tjap so that the pattern would repeat and also could be used on a 90° angle corner—for example on a scarf. The tjaps used in Indonesia are much more complicated, often with very beautiful and delicate designs. When designing one's own it is as well to keep to simple lines.

The tjanting is not an easy tool to use at first but it is worthwhile persevering with as it is the most satisfactory tool for producing fine and more precise designs. The tjanting is dipped into the tin or pan containing the hot wax to fill the reservoir. The skill is in carrying the tjanting to the cloth without dripping the wax in the wrong place. If one holds a piece of cloth or paper under the spout and masks the area of work which is not being dealt

Fabric Printing and Dyeing at Home

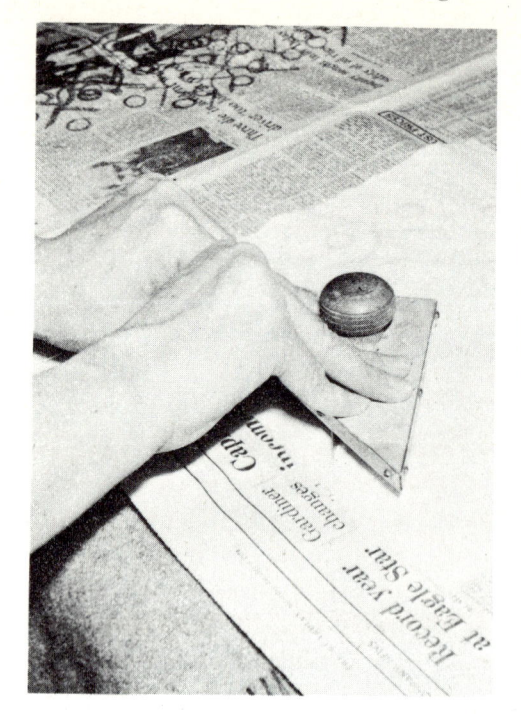

Figure 63. Here we see the tjap (with the hot wax on the edges of the design) being pressed firmly onto a piece of cloth. The cloth is laid on newspaper, underneath which are two layers of an old blanket. The blanket makes a soft foundation to press the tjap onto and the pattern will come out more clearly than if only newspaper was used on the worksurface.

with at the time, one should be able to avoid misplaced blobs. Practice will soon bring facility with this tool. It will appeal particularly to people who are gifted or experienced in drawing, as, to get best results, one needs to work with quick, certain, yet free strokes.

Brushes

Wax can easily be applied with ordinary paint brushes and they can be used to fill in large areas and to make spots and lines.

It is usual, although not absolutely necessary, to begin with the palest colour and as each subsequent colour is added the cloth becomes darker, resulting in a light design on a dark background.

It is possible, however, to begin by waxing the background part of the design and leaving the main motif unwaxed to receive the dye.

One of the most attractive characteristics of Batik work is the fine network of lines of colour which appear when the dye enters through cracks in the wax. Candle-wax is a hard and brittle wax and will give many cracks. If less crackle is desired the candle wax may be made softer by adding beeswax in proportion 1:4 by weight.

Wax–Resist Batik

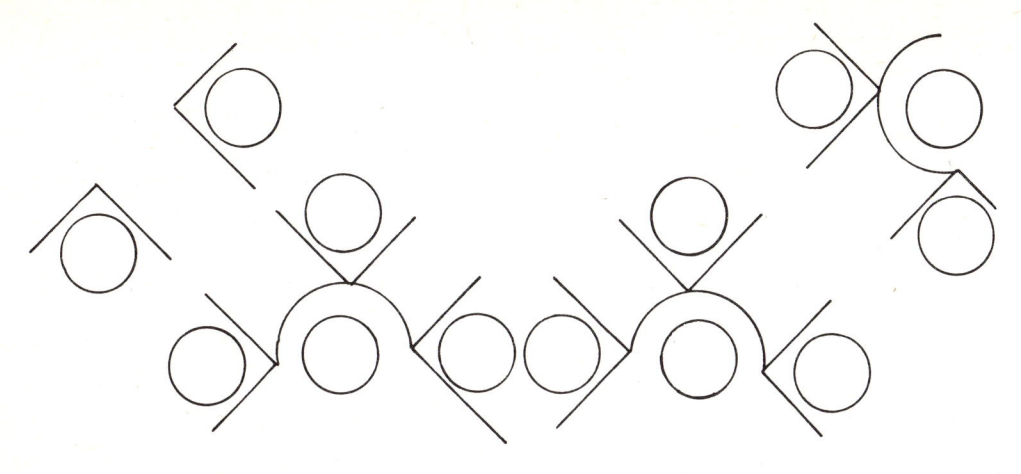

Figure 64. This line illustration shows how a simple geometric design with angles of 90° and 45° will fit together to make a border pattern.

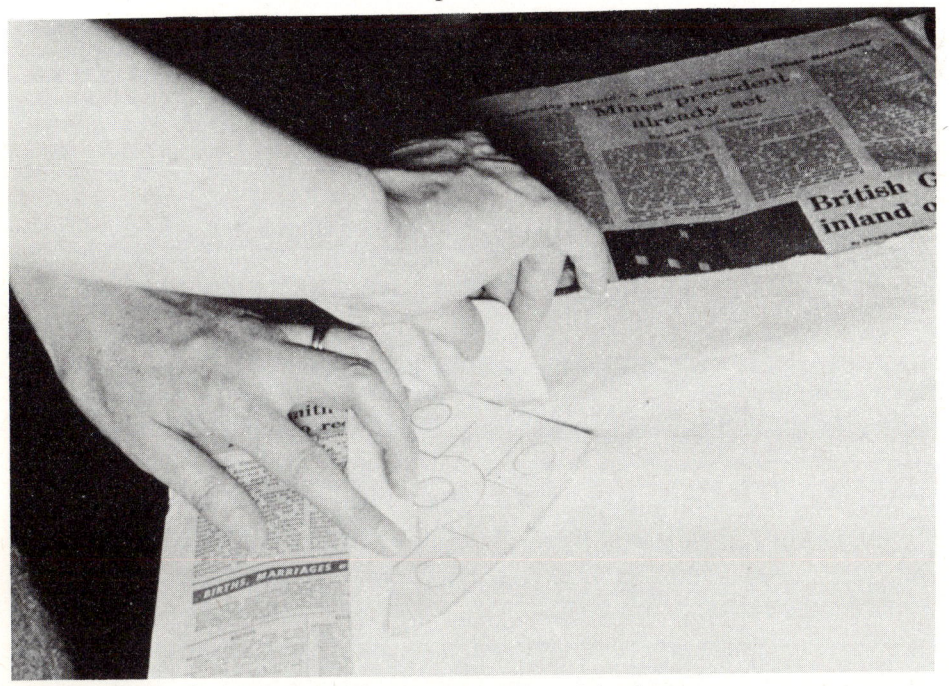

Figure 65. A paper template of the design is outlined with tailor's chalk; this acts as a guide when using the tjap.

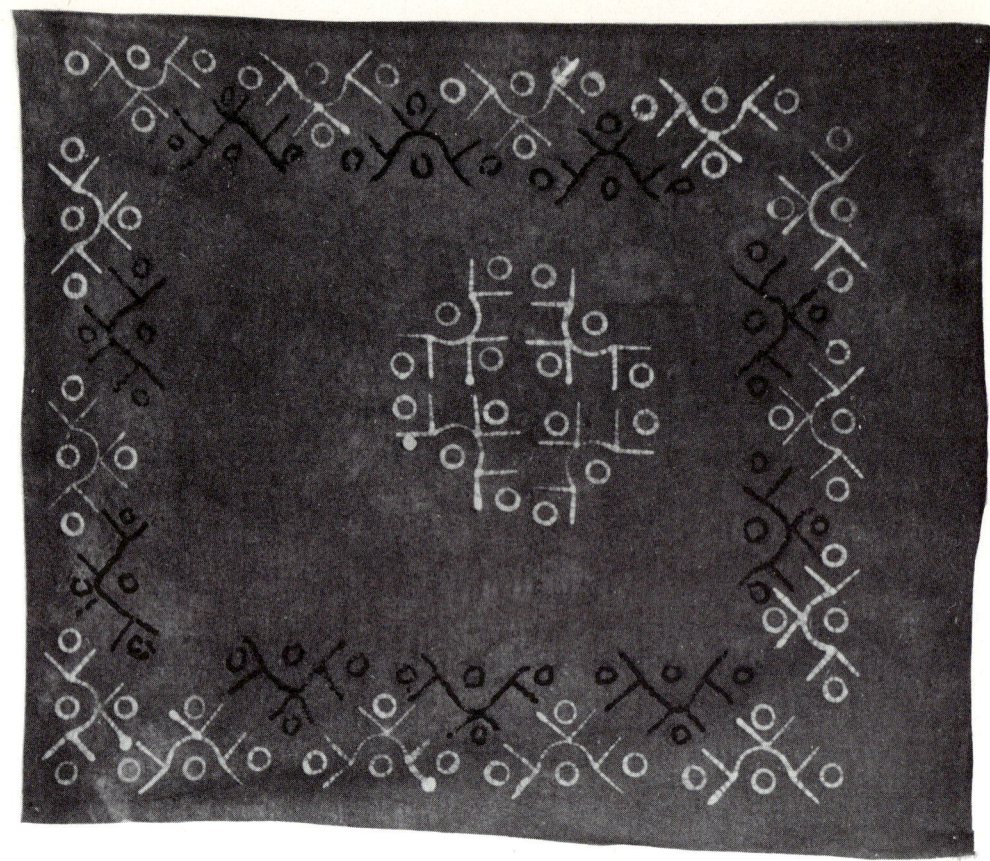

Figure 66. The cloth is waxed once and is then dyed and the wax boiled off.

2 DYEING THE FABRIC

As the wax must be kept cold whilst dyeing only cold dyes should be used.

3 FIXING THE DYE

A method of fixing the dye for use with wax batik is to lay out the fabric as flat as possible in a slightly warm, moist or steamy atmosphere for twenty-four hours. The kitchen or bathroom or even a greenhouse would be ideal. Lay the cloth, unrinsed, on several layers of newspaper which have been backed with plastic sheet or polythene. It will not hurt to fold the fabric if it is a large sample. This warm, moist atmosphere will be sufficient to fix the dye. After twenty-four hours, and when the cloth is dry, a second

Wax–Resist Batik

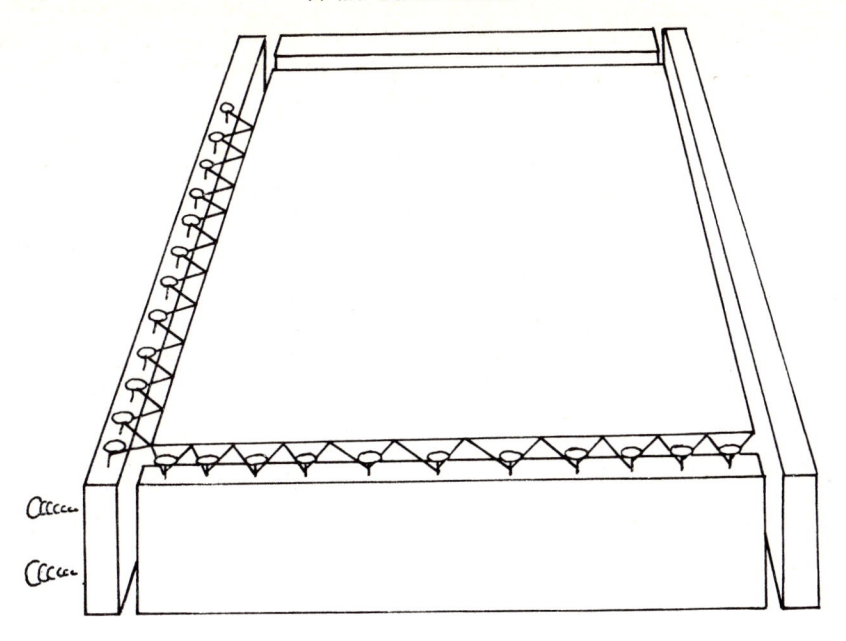

Figure 67. A 27″ (68 cm) wooden frame for batik work. METHOD: Four pieces of wood measuring 2″ x 1″ x 27″ are screwed together. Tacks are knocked in at 1″ intervals, leaving the heads sticking up. The cloth is tacked on with a needle and each stitch thread slipped round a tack. In this way it can be removed from the frame for dyeing and put back for further waxing by simply 'unhooking' the stitches from the tack heads, without undoing them.

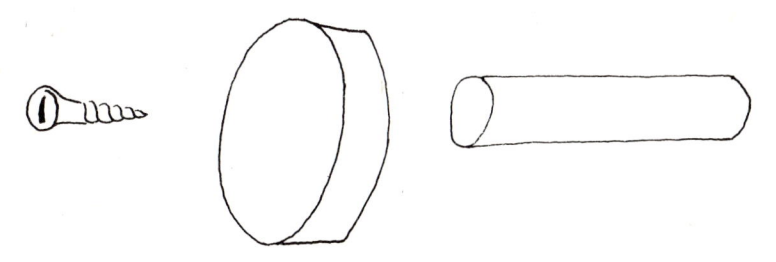

Figure 68. Tin lid mounted on a piece of broom handle.

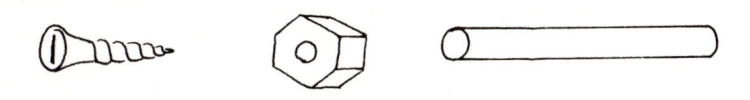

Figure 69. Hexagonal nut mounted on a piece of dowel rod.

Fabric Printing and Dyeing at Home

Figure 70. The tjanting in use. Notice that it is being held in a different way to Figure 60. Some people find they have more control with this hold. METHOD: A wooden frame 27" sq. has been made to hold the cloth away from the paper beneath it. If the hot wax soaked through the cloth directly onto the newspaper, it would cause the two to stick together, and the wax would crack and break when the paper was pulled away. If one does not wish to use a wooden frame and prefers to lay the cloth directly on newspaper, the area of the cloth being worked on must be lifted by hand as the wax is applied; as soon as the wax has cooled—in a few seconds—it may be laid down and work proceed on the next part. The lightest part of this pattern is wax that was applied when the cloth was white; the cloth was taken off the frame and dyed light blue. The cloth is put back on the frame and more wax applied; in Figure 70 these show as darker parts as the wax makes the cloth appear to be transparent.

application of wax may be added and the fabric dyed a second time; this time in a darker colour. After being dyed twice the wax will begin to deteriorate due to the alkaline nature of the dye, and it will have to be washed off. When dry it will be possible to apply another two coats of wax and dye if desired.

4 REMOVING THE WAX

First rinse the cloth thoroughly in cold water to remove excess dye. Choose a pan or pail large enough to hold the cloth and to allow its free movement when water is added. Heat the water to boiling ($212°F/100°C$); plunge the cloth in and stir it with a wooden stick for 2–3 minutes. Before removing the cloth, and wearing rubber gloves, press it into a small and compact ball, quickly bring it out of the hot water and plunge it into a bowl of cold water.

Wax–Resist Batik

Some of the wax will be left in the hot water and more will immediately harden on the surface of the cold water; yet more will still cling to the cloth and this should be easy to shake off. As the wax hardens it may be collected up for re-use, and in any case the hot wax should *not* be poured down the sink or

Figure 71. Some other ways of applying the wax to the cloth. Art brushes of different thicknesses may be used; any kind of metal tubes such as the Steradent container. Plastic cotton reels make pretty shapes but the plastic does become misshapen after being used a few times; also shown are pins stuck into a cork which make a dotted design. Tin lids mounted on a piece of broom-handle (Figure 68) or hexagonal nuts mounted on dowel rod (Figure 69) all make useful stamps.

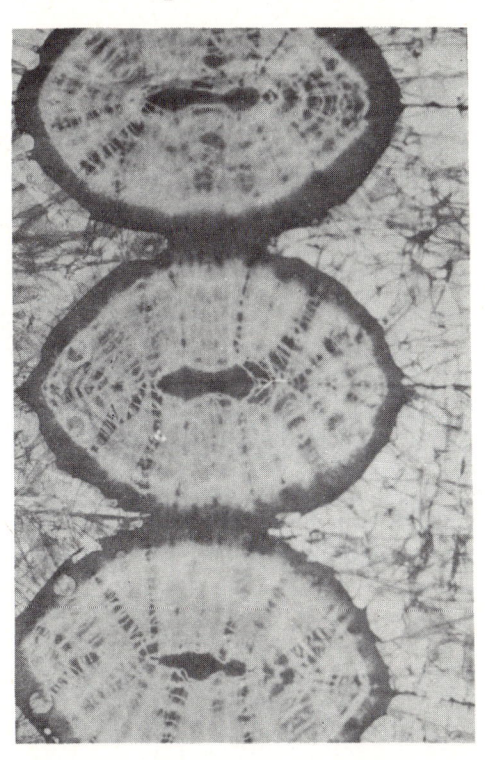

Figure 72. This length of cloth has been patterned using both tie and dye and batik methods. A patterned cloth with a considerable amount of white in it was required for use as a lampshade. METHOD: Tie and dye ovals are stitched and bound with string, and the entire background is painted with hot liquid wax, which, after cooling, is crumpled to create the 'crackle' effect of fine lines. The cloth is next dyed a rose-red. After untying and boiling off the wax, the end result is an attractively patterned cloth with enough white areas to allow light to shine through.

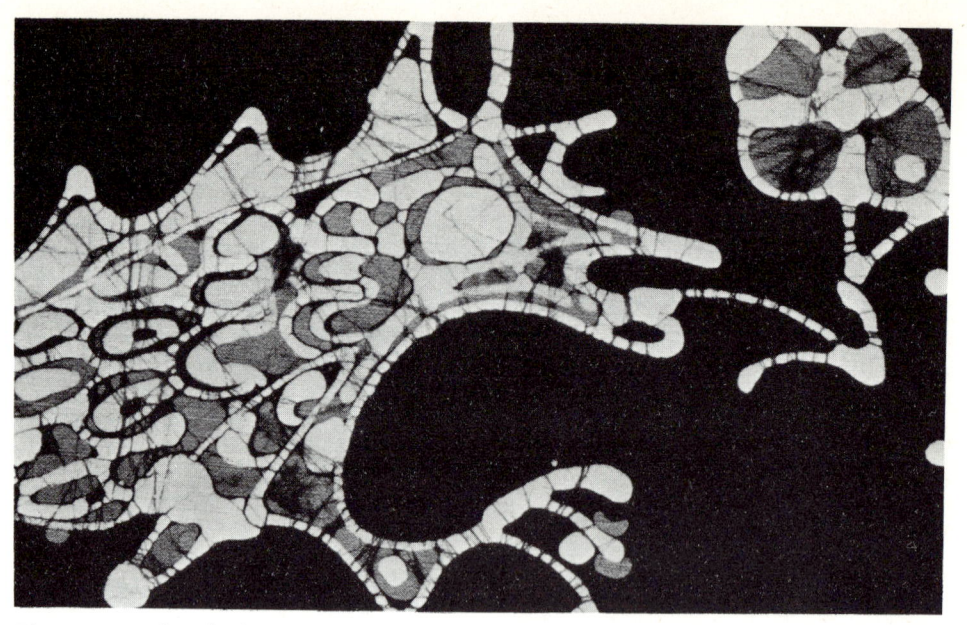

Figure 73. This freehand 'dragon' was outlined in hot wax, following which the cloth was dyed yellow. After further applications of wax the cloth was again dyed, this time in a pale shade of blue. The parts of the cloth which remained unwaxed then became green. Further wax was applied, and the whole dyed a dark red. As most of the cloth was green in colour the red dye on the top produced a dark wine shade. The final result is shown on the cover of this book.

it may harden in the waste pipe. The process may be repeated with the addition of half a teaspoon of Lissapol to the water. Then wash the cloth in warm soapy water. If the cloth is then ironed between blotting paper or newspaper any last traces of wax will be removed.

Equipment for Wax Batik

A double saucepan or a tin stood in a saucepan of water
A sugar boiling thermometer if available
A simple wooden frame as illustrated
An old blanket, layers of newspaper
Candles, or paraffin wax. Beeswax is optional
Tjanting, paint brushes and home-made stamps in variety
Home made tjap if possible
Rubber gloves
Plastic bowls and/or buckets

3

Flour-Resist Batik

In parts of Africa and Java, resist patterns are made on cloth with a paste made from the cassava plant and water. Some European books on fabric printing suggest making a similar paste by boiling ordinary flour with laundry starch. However, the writer has found that household flour, plain or self-raising, will make a perfectly satisfactory paste when mixed with cold water. The paste should be of a consistency to drop easily from the prongs of a fork and yet not be too runny. If one makes a few tests on a spare scrap of cloth it will soon be possible to gauge the correct thickness.

The flour paste can be applied in several different ways and has some advantages over wax-resist. The advantages are that one can take more time over patterns and designs, as there is no need to hurry before the flour paste hardens, which one must do with wax. More detailed and controlled designs can be produced and repeat designs will be more accurate. Also one can make repeat patterns with stencils, which is useful; sometimes a variety of different stencils can be used to make up one large design motif.

The methods of application are with a plastic detergent bottle, a slip trailer or a plastic disposable syringe, obtainable from chemists. These three articles are useful for making lines and dots and give similar results to a tjanting. The design is marked lightly on the cloth with chalk and then followed in a similar manner to icing a cake.

Stencils may be cut out of Vinolay tiles with a craft knife. These Vinolay stencils are very satisfactory as they are strong and durable. They must be rinsed and dried after each application otherwise the flour paste will get on the underside of the stencil and mark the cloth. It is better to have the flour

Fabric Printing and Dyeing at Home

Figure 74. Flour paste being applied with a slip trailer. This is ideal for line or dot designs and it can be used for filling in larger areas. The bulb is made of flexible rubber and the nozzle of rigid plastic. It is simple to load a slip trailer with paste: pull the rigid nozzle out of the rubber bulb, press as much air out of the bulb as possible and hold the aperture against the surface of the flour paste. When the pressure on the bulb is released the suction will pull the paste into the bulb. Repeat this two or three times until the bulb is full. Replace the nozzle and the slip trailer is ready for use.

Figure 75. A disposable syringe can also be used for making lines in flour paste but it is not so easy to fill. However, if one also has a slip trailer, this can be used to fill the syringe. Another alternative is a plastic washing-up liquid bottle. Remove the nozzle, pour the flour paste in through a funnel, and then replace the nozzle.

Flour–Resist Batik

Figure 76. Mrs. Middleton, Women's Institute member at Denman College, brushes Procion dye, thickened with Manutex R.S., over flour-resist batik work.

Fabric Printing and Dyeing at Home

This shape cut out with craft knife

Figure 77

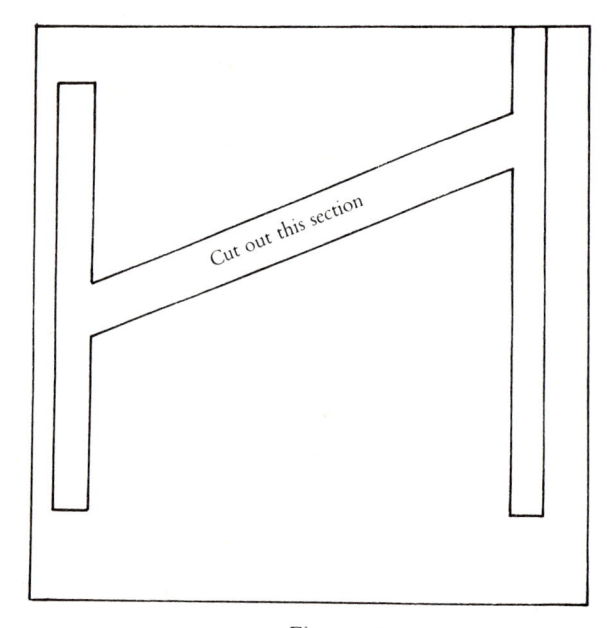

Cut out this section

Figure 78

▶ *Opposite page:*
Figure 79. Close-up of a length of flour-resist material. This design is inspired by an Aztec pattern and has been freely adapted. METHOD: The cloth is dyed a plain pale green as the first step. Next, stencils are cut in a vinolay tile. Flour paste is brushed into these shapes and thickened dye brushed over when the dye is dry. Some parts of the design are painted separately. When finished, the whole of the cloth is covered with flour paste from edge to edge. As soon as this is dry the paste is crackled and thickened dye in a dark colour is brushed into the cracks. The dye is fixed and paste washed off according to instructions.

Flour–Resist Batik

paste slightly thicker than for slip trailers, and the paste is best applied with a small spoon into large parts of the design and then pushed into the finer parts with a finger. Brushes are not satisfactory for applying flour paste and they are very difficult to get thoroughly clean after use. Large areas of flour paste may have patterns scraped or combed into them whilst the paste is still wet.

When the flour paste dries it will contract a little, causing the surrounding material to pucker. When it is thoroughly dry the material may be gently stretched back to shape and cracks will appear in the paste; these will allow dye to penetrate, giving an attractive crackle effect very similar to that obtained with wax batik. The paste may be applied all over a piece of cloth, and when dry the cloth may be crumpled and stretched to make an all-over crackle effect possible. This is a useful background for a more detailed design to be printed on to, or to go on top of, a design which needs 'unifying' with a darker or stronger colour. It is also a very attractive way to lightly pattern fine material for making up into lampshades (see note).

DYEING FLOUR-RESIST BATIK

As one applies the flour paste it quickly becomes apparent that one cannot dye the cloth in the same way as for wax batik. There are two reasons for

Fabric Printing and Dyeing at Home

this. One is that the resist is only on one side of the cloth instead of having penetrated right into it as with wax-resist. Therefore the dye would take all over the other side of the cloth and there would be no pattern. The other reason is that the paste would soften and disintegrate if it was put into a liquid dye bath.

Fortunately there is a simple solution to this problem. Procion Dye can be thickened and then brushed onto the fabric. It can be worked into the cracks in the flour paste to enhance the crackle effect or worked round it if no crackle is desired. For large areas of cloth a sponge roller may be used to apply it.

THICKENING PROCION DYE

This method is for use in flour-resist, also for string block printing and free hand painting. This thickened dye may also be used over wax batik. Some types of dye thickening leave the cloth rather stiff but this combination of Procion and Manutex leaves the cloth with exactly the same feel or 'handle' as it originally had, as the Manutex washes out easily and completely.

Figure 80. The thickened dye solution is prepared according to the instructions given on page 50.

Flour–Resist Batik

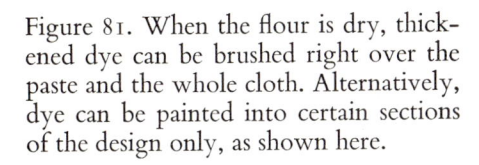

Figure 81. When the flour is dry, thickened dye can be brushed right over the paste and the whole cloth. Alternatively, dye can be painted into certain sections of the design only, as shown here.

Figure 82. A cockerel design and border outlined in flour paste on light grey cloth. When dry, green dye paste was brushed into parts of the design.

Recipe for thickened Procion dye:

Put 1 tsp. of Calgon in 1 pint water.

Sprinkle 1 level tbsp. Manutex R.S. If possible beat with household mixer. Leave until transparent.

In another jar put 10 parts (10 level tsps.) urea dissolved in 45 parts (10 level tbsps.) water. This solution is then stirred into either 20 parts (5 tbsps.) of the Manutex if a thin paste is required for batik work or painting, or 40 parts (10 tbsps.) if a thicker paste is required for block printing; then add one part (1 tsp.) (Resist Salt L).

The bicarbonate of soda is not added until immediately before use.

The required shade and/or colour of Procion dye may be added in quite small quantities, say $\frac{1}{4}$ tsp. up to 5 or 6 tsps. to whatever amount of printing

Figure 83. The design for this panel of flour-resist batik is taken from Jorge Enciso's *Design Motifs of Ancient Mexico*. METHOD: A piece of cloth is dyed a plain lemon yellow. The serpents are then applied in flour paste, using a disposable syringe (see Figure 75). When the flour is dry, yellow and a little red Procion dye are mixed to make a salmon shade. This is thickened with Manutex R.S. and brushed over the whole of the cloth. The lightest parts of the border design are then created with the flour paste and a disposable syringe. When this is dry, red thickened dye is brushed over the whole. Further flour paste is applied to the border design and then a very dark brownish red is brushed onto the border only. When dry, the cloth is wrapped in newspaper and baked for 5 minutes at 285°F to fix the dye. The flour paste is removed in cold water, a spoon being used to scrape it off.

paste is estimated to be necessary. (This printing paste will keep for several weeks if stored in the dark). For small amounts of printing paste stir in $\frac{1}{4}$ tsp. bicarbonate after adding the dye and just before use; for the larger amounts necessary for large pieces of work stir in $1\frac{1}{2}$ parts ($1\frac{1}{2}$ tsps.) bicarbonate of soda.

The dye is only active for about 4 hours once the bicarbonate has been added.

When the dye is dry, further additions of flour paste may be made and then further applications of dye. It is usual to apply paler and lighter shades of dye first, building up to darker tones.

The sample may be fixed by baking or ironing as described on page 50.

Equipment for Flour-Resist Batik

Plastic detergent bottles
Syringes, Slip trailers
Vinolay tiles
Craft knives
Paint brushes for the thickened dye
Newspaper, Polythene
Iron and ironing board
Pots or jars of various sizes
A kitchen mixer, either hand or electric, is useful but not essential

4

String Block Printing

String block printing is a discharge method; that is to say, the dye is applied in a pattern rather than kept off the fabric in a pattern as in batik and tie and dye.

It is a very useful method of patterning, either to use on its own or to supplement other forms of dyeing; it can be used to give detail and emphasis to more generalized patterns either, or both, in colour and line.

Wooden blocks about $\frac{1}{2}''$ thick and $1''$ square are a convenient size for beginning. String about $\frac{3}{8}''$ thick is better than anything too thin. Evo-stick is painted over the wood on one side and allowed to become tacky; the string is then pressed into place in the predetermined pattern. The string should be made of an absorbent natural fibre—not nylon or man-made.

The printing pad for the dye is simply a piece of plastic foam on a tin plate with thickened dye (see recipe for flour-resist batik) poured on. The dye must, of course, be activated with bicarbonate of soda and may be fixed by baking or ironing as in batik work.

The amount of dye used in the thickening may need to be increased to the larger amount—5 teaspoons to achieve a really strong colour. This is because the dye paste does not penetrate into the cloth so readily in this form of printing as when it can be worked in with a paint brush. The results will depend on the type and weave of material used and tests should be made on a small sample before beginning a serious piece of work.

String Block Printing

Figure 84. Simple 'leaf' and 'petal' shapes cut out of $\frac{1}{2}''$ plywood. The shapes have been repeated in newspaper and these will be used to plan a design as they can easily be rearranged and moved about to try out different effects. Some of the blocks have the string stuck on them.

When using string blocks to supplement other types of fabric printing the design of the block will of course relate to the work already carried out. It may be that something very simple in shape—merely a few lines or a circle or two but in a contrasting colour—will be all that is needed to bring an otherwise 'ordinary' piece of tie and dye or batik work to life. This is often the field where string-block printing will have a considerable value.

Some people prefer to take the purist view and not mix methods and techniques, believing that each method should be able to stand on its own merits; but it is finally up to the individual to follow and develop her own taste and is indeed all 'part of the fun' of creative fabric dyeing.

An alternative type of printing pad to that shown in Figure 86 may be made by stapling two or three layers of woollen blanket round a block of

Fabric Printing and Dyeing at Home

Figure 85. Mounting string on the block. METHOD: Evo-stick is spread over the wood and allowed to become tacky, which takes about ten minutes. String is firmly pressed onto the Evo-stick and will remain in place. The string should be cut with a craft-knife blade rather than scissors, which tend to fray the edges.

wood. If the wood is about 5" or 6" square and 1" thick that would be a convenient size. The dye paste should be worked into the blanket with a spoon before beginning to print. This type of pad, being firmer, should give a more even and reliable print than the plastic foam though it takes a little more trouble to prepare.

The cloth being printed should be ironed and completely crease-free. The newspaper should be firmly fixed to the blanket with pins or masking tape and then the cloth fixed to the paper with tape. This will prevent any movement and make it much simpler to keep to the design plan. When printing is finished take care, when moving the cloth, not to smudge or blot the work. Ideally it should be left to dry before being moved. A second colour may be printed when the first is quite dry though it could be an

String Block Printing

Figure 86. Simple printing pad made with a piece of plastic foam on an enamel plate. The Manutex thickening is made up as described on page 50 and activated with bicarbonate of soda.

Figure 87. When the thickened dye has been mixed and has been worked into the foam pad with the back of a spoon it is ready for use. The prepared block is lightly pressed onto the pad. Practise by printing onto newspaper first. If too much dye is picked up on some parts of the block, the surplus between the string may be wiped away with a scrap of cloth.

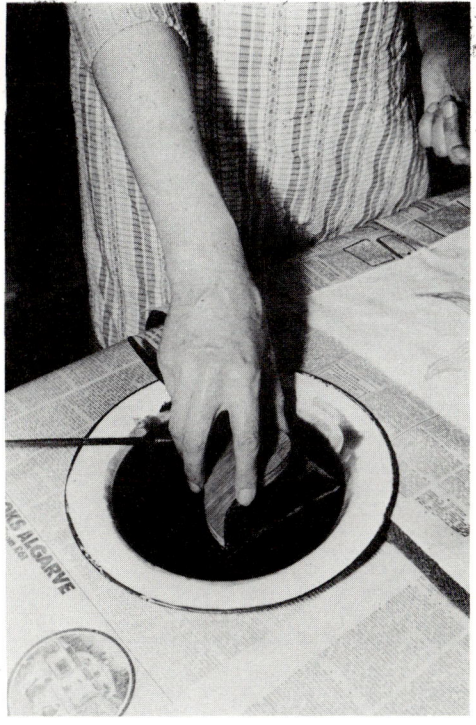

Figure 88. One of the leaf blocks being used: it must be pressed quite firmly with the fingers. The cloth is laid on newspaper covering two thicknesses of blanket; thus providing a soft yet firm foundation to print on.

advantage to fix by baking and to wash-off the loose dye before proceeding to subsequent colours. This is because the colour may become paler and less distinct after washing away the thickening—see note on p.52. This is an important point to remember about string block printing.

String Block Printing

Figure 89. Design for a cushion. METHOD: The cloth is first dyed a plain yellow, then paper shapes are pinned in place and thick dye brushed over them. The light circles are covered and orange dye brushed all over, then more circles and alternate leaves are pinned on and red dye brushed all over these. With all the paper shapes in place, a dark purplish red is used as a background colour. Finally, the string-block shapes are printed onto the lighter backgrounds. The dye is fixed by baking for 5 minutes at 285°F after each application; the cloth is then washed thoroughly to remove the thickening, dried and ironed.

Fabric Printing and Dyeing at Home

Equipment for String Block Printing

Wooden blocks ½″ thick and any convenient size ranging from 1″ square to 1″ x 2″–2″ square
Evo-stick
Foam plastic sponge, tin plate or similar
Masking tape
Piece of blanket

Opposite page: ▶
Figures 90 and 91. This Women's Institute member at Denman College has designed an attractive string-block and is trying it out. She is using thickened Procion dye with a thin piece of plastic foam on a plate as a printing pad.

String Block Printing

Figure 90

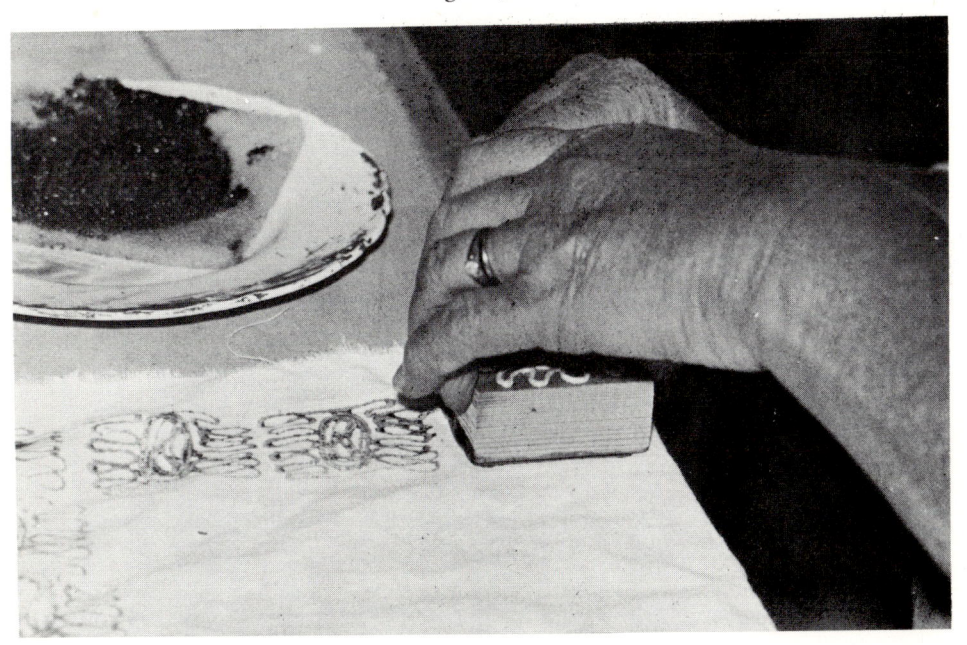

Figure 91

59

5

Lino Printing

Lino printing is an exciting method of fabric printing with great scope for imagination and creativity. It can be used to make quite simple designs such as children might use or ones of great sophistication. Essentially, lino printing is a 'discharge' process in which dye is put *onto* the cloth, as in string block printing. (As we have seen, tie and dye and batik are 'resist' methods where the pattern is created by keeping the dye *off* the material in chosen areas.)

As a supplement to resist methods it can add emphasis and strength to otherwise mediocre designs and can be used to bring strongly contrasting colours into an otherwise harmonious scheme. This is not usually possible in the resist methods, when successive dyeings on top of each other tend to blend rather than contrast.

When using lino or string block printing to supplement the other methods, care and discrimination are necessary. One would not wish to end up with a hotch-potch of methods which could all tend to distract from each other. However, with a little thought and experiment it can be very valuable as a supplement in this field. A good guiding rule would be to have about 90% of the design made up in one technique, with not more than 5% in either lino or string block printing.

Lino printing on fabric can of course be used entirely on its own as a method of fabric printing, and in this case it would be usual to use it as a repeat pattern to build up into borders and or edges or all-over designs.

Small pieces of lino, say 3" x 3", mounted on a backing of plywood, are the most suitable for a beginning. Evo-stick is a good adhesive for this purpose. Start with a simple pattern to get the feel of the tools and the effect

Lino Printing

Figure 92. Simple design motif on a 3" square block of lino. All the white parts are cut away leaving the shaded areas standing above the background. This is then coated with flocking powder and will print the shaded part onto cloth just as it appears in the diagram.

of the print. If the lino is warmed slightly it will cut more easily. It will be the part of the lino which is not cut away that will print so it is rather like cutting a negative of the pattern. One must leave behind a clearly outlined design, cutting away all the spaces in between and around the pattern. First draw a design on the lino with pencil. If it is difficult to see the pencil marks, paint the lino with a light coloured distemper first.

Use a narrow cutting vee tool to outline the design, remembering to leave a clean sharp edge. This may seem difficult at first but with practice it becomes quite easy. It may be found better to move the block under the tool, keeping the tool itself almost stationary. Once the design has been outlined with the narrow vee tool then the main areas can be cut away with the U-shaped tool.

After the pattern has been cut you must make the lino block more absorbent to the dye by flocking it. Spread the special adhesive known as

Fabric Printing and Dyeing at Home

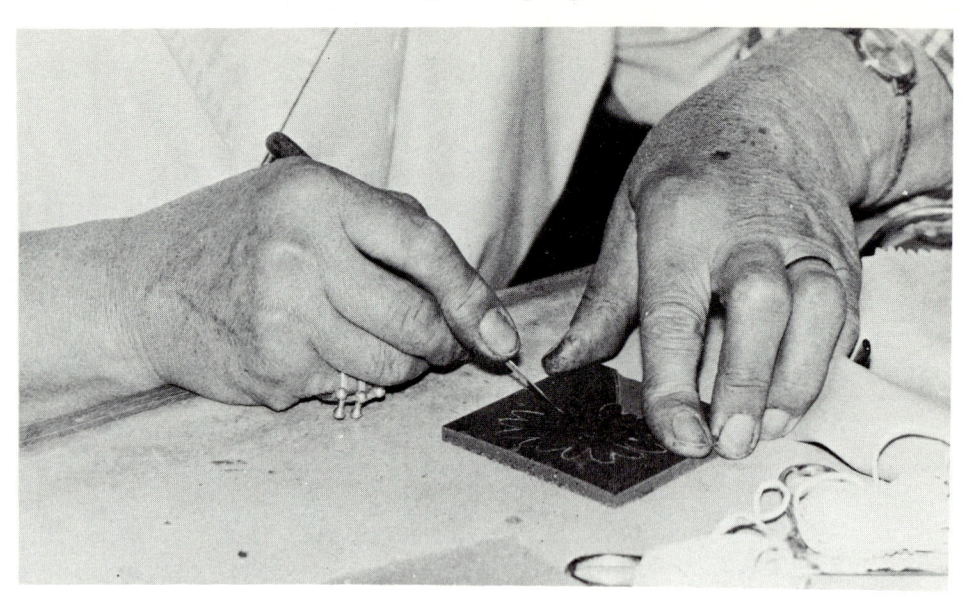

Figure 93. After outlining the design with a narrow vee tool, the main areas are cut away with a U-shaped tool.

'flocking mordant' thinly and evenly over the lino, taking care to leave no thin patches; then sprinkle the flocking powder generously over the mordant and leave for 24 hours. The surplus flocking powder may be then shaken off and may be reserved for future use; the block is now ready for printing. If after some use the flocking wears thin, it can be sandpapered off and re-treated and after 24 hours is ready for use again.

The printing pad as used for string block is quite satisfactory for lino printing. A little experimenting will teach the best density for the Manutex thickening; if it is too thick it may blur the design. The colour strength, too, may need testing; if the Manutex is too thick it may not hold enough colour to yield the desired strength. The purpose of the Manutex thickening is, after all, to act as a vehicle for the dye and to control its flow. The ideal is to have it thick enough to prevent the dye running off the edge of the block but not so thick as to fill the design and therefore smudge it, or to make the final colour result too pale and weak.

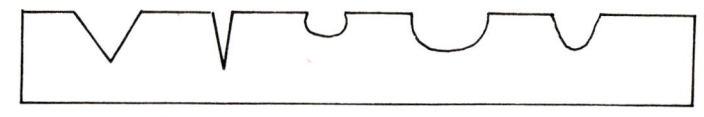

Figure 94. Section of linoleum illustrating the differently shaped cuts obtainable.

Equipment for Lino Printing

Lino: purchased already mounted or one can mount one's own
Wood to mount lino, $\frac{1}{4}''$ plywood for small blocks, $\frac{1}{2}''$ for larger
Evo-stick
Lino cutting handle and a variety of nibs
Nib remover
Flocking mordant
Flocking powder
Procion Dyes
Manutex thickening as used in String Block Printing and Flour-Resist batik
Printing pad as used in String Block Printing (see Figure 86)

Figure 95. Panel produced by folding the fabric asymmetrically and stitching the shapes through all the layers together before gathering. Two colours were used but during the red dyeing the other areas were protected.

6

Dye Recipes and Methods

Dylon cold dyes are admirable for batik and tie and dye; they are fast to washing and to sunlight, their colours are now available in quite a good range and they may be intermixed with one another and also with Procion 'M' Range of dyes. It is strongly recommended that these dyes should be used for first attempts. However, for those who wish to practise the craft over some period of time, it is more exciting to buy a few basic colours in larger quantities and mix one's own exact choice of shade and colour. For this purpose Procion 'M' Range is the ideal dye to choose. Only five basic colours are necessary to make a start:

Yellow	MX	6GS
Yellow	MX	4RS
Red	MX	8BS
Blue	MX	3GS
Blue	MX	RB

These Procion 'M' dyes are stronger and more concentrated than Dylon Cold dyes, therefore less dye is used. The number of shades and tones are infinitely variable and Procion dyes are 100% fast to washing and sunlight. This last quality is essential: it would be most disappointing to spend a good deal of time and trouble on a piece of work, only to see its brilliance fade subsequently.

There are a number of different recipes and methods for using Procion. The essential things to remember are: (a) that the dye begins to react as soon as, and not before, the sodium bicarbonate (washing-soda or Salsoda in the USA) is added; (b) that the dye needs some form of fixing once it has been

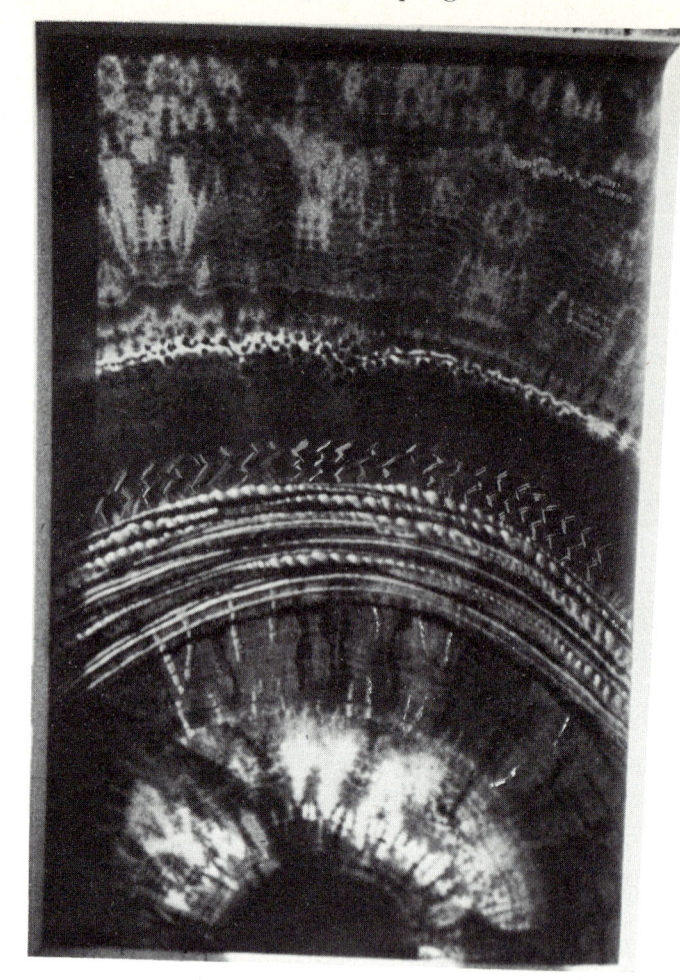

Figure 96. A dip-dyed panel in simple open binding with areas defined by lines of stitching. Couching and hand stitching have been added to the bands across the middle of the panel.

applied to the cloth. The fixing method will vary according to the method of fabric printing that is being used.

Lissapol is the washing soap recommended by the makers of Procion Dyes but the writer has found that any good quality household washing powder is satisfactory. A certain amount of loose dye will always come out of the material after fixing the dye; this is quite natural and to be expected. Provided that the fixing process was carried out accurately it should all wash away and the dyes will be fast to further washings. It is important that the fabric should be washed and rinsed thoroughly until the water runs clear after each fixing process, otherwise muddy colours may result.

RECIPE AND METHOD FOR PROCION 'M' AND DYLON COLD, FOR WAX RESIST AND TIE AND DYE

The following will dye about 2–3 yards according to weight and thickness of the cloth:

      1 teaspoon Procion 'M' dye
      or 1 tin Dylon Cold (i.e. 10 grammes or 2 teaspoons)
      4 tablespoons salt
      1 tablespoon washing soda (Salsoda, USA)
      2 pints (Imperial) water (1 litre)

Paste the dye in a little warm water and then make up to one pint with cold water. Dissolve the salt in $\frac{1}{2}$ pint water and add to the dye mixture. A plastic bucket or bowl is an ideal vessel to use; dissolve the washing soda in the remaining $\frac{1}{2}$ pint water and allow it to cool; reserve this soda solution on one side for the time being.

For tie and dye the sample should be rinsed out in a solution of acetic acid (as described on page 69) before dyeing. For wax-batik the dye solution must be quite cold so as not to soften the wax, but the temperature may be 70°C (160°F) for tie and dye work.

Place the fabric in the dye for 3–4 minutes, ensuring even immersion under the liquid. The dye will not begin to react onto the cloth at this stage as the soda has not been added. Remove the cloth and stir in the soda solution, then replace the cloth in the dye for at least 20 minutes, and wearing rubber gloves, keep the fabric moving under the dye for the first ten minutes. The main strength of the dye will be transferred to the cloth within the first 20 minutes but the cloth may be left in the dye for several hours or even overnight. The cloth should be stirred and turned from time to time and may be kept under the surface of the dye with a sheet of plastic which is weighted down with heavy objects.

ALTERNATIVE RECIPE AND METHOD FOR PROCION DYESTUFF*

Weigh out 7 gm. ($\frac{1}{4}$ oz) dye
90–100 gm. ($3\frac{1}{2}$ oz) common salt
21 gm. ($\frac{3}{4}$ oz) common soda (Salsoda USA)
1–2 litres (2–3 Imperial pints) of soft water

Method
1. Paste the dye with a little cold water
2. Add about $\frac{1}{4}$ litre ($\frac{1}{2}$ pint) warm water—not above 70°C (160°F) and stir well so that a clear solution is obtained
3. Add the rest of the cold, soft water $\frac{3}{4}$ litre–$1\frac{3}{4}$ litres ($1\frac{1}{2}$–$2\frac{1}{2}$ pints)
4. Add 90–100 gm. ($3\frac{1}{2}$ oz) common salt and stir
5. Immerse sample in dye for 3 to 5 minutes
6. Add 21 gm. ($\frac{3}{4}$ oz) common soda (Salsoda, USA) dissolved in a little water and stir
7. Dye for a further 15 minutes or as long as possible
8. Lift sample and squeeze out surplus dye into dyebath
9. The colour is much more powerful if the following process can be added:
   (a) Wrap sample in a cloth or newspaper and bake in an oven for 5 to 10 minutes at 140°C (285°F or Regulo 1);
   OR
   (b) Wrap sample, place in a basin and steam in a saucepan for 10 minutes
10. If possible leave overnight before rinsing, drying and untying
11. After untying, wash sample in hot soapy water for 5–15 minutes. Lissapol is recommended for this in the proportion 1–2 parts Lissapol to 1,000 water.

Procion dyes take well on all natural fibres, particularly on mercerized cotton or poplin and all other cotton cloths, pure linen or cotton/linen mixtures and pure wool; they also take well on pure silk, but the colours are softer and less brilliant and strong than on cotton. For tying and dyeing, cotton velvet and towelling may be used also. Cellulose fibres, e.g. viscose rayon, which are made from wood pulp and are, therefore, really 'natural' fibres, will take the dye but not man-made nylons and Terylenes, etc. When buying material for any fabric dyeing, one should ask for a small sample and test it unless one is absolutely sure it is a natural fibre. Cloths which have

* For further technical information on Procion dyes see *An Introduction to Textile Printing* published by Butterworth in Association with I.C.I. Dyestuffs Division.

been treated with crease-resistant or flame-resistant finishes should be tested too. The cloth should always be thoroughly washed before use and, although one should take care when washing wool, Jap silk can be boiled for a few minutes in a mild detergent; plain cottons of course will wash in the normal way. It is not recommended to use wool for wax batik because the hot water and/or ironing necessary to remove the wax may shrink the cloth.

The strength of the colour may be varied by using more or less dye. It is not necessary to alter the amount of soda and salt, etc., unless one is multiplying the whole recipe to dye a proportionately larger piece of cloth.

Do not attempt to make the dye paler by adding more water. Instead use *less* dye.

If you wish to dye two identical pieces of cloth, e.g. a pair of curtains or a set of table mats, they must either all be immersed in the dye together at one and the same time or fresh dye must be carefully weighed out for subsequent pieces. If the samples are added one after another the dye will be progressively paler with each piece, although the appearance of the liquid will remain the same. Finally the dye will no longer give colour at all and then the dye is said to be 'exhausted'.

The maximum temperature to which Procion may be heated is 160°F/70°C.

USE OF PROCION FOR TIE AND DYE WORK ONLY

A characteristic of Procion is its great power of penetration; this at first sight makes it seem unsuitable for tie and dye work, as, without certain precautions, it can penetrate under even the tightest tying. However, because Procion cannot tolerate acid, this difficulty is soon overcome. When the tie and dye work is tied and ready for dyeing, it should be rinsed out in a solution of acetic acid and cool water in the proportions of 2 teaspoons of acetic acid (which is easily obtained and non-poisonous) to 2 pints of water. The cloth may be simply squeezed or wrung tightly with the hands and then put into a solution of bicarbonate of soda—4 teaspoons to 2 pints of cool water. This soda solution has the effect of neutralizing the acid on the untied areas and the dye will take on those areas; but the acid will be retained under the string and stitching and so will make the resist pattern more clearly defined. After this process dyeing may proceed with any of the methods given and any convenient method of fixing may be used for tie and dye.

Here are two methods of fixing Procion Dye suitable for flour-resist batik and string block printing (but *not* for wax batik). Method 1 is suitable for tie and dye.

1. After the fabric has been dyed, the cloth may still be wet with dye, but *without rinsing*, wrap the cloth loosely in newspaper or cloth and bake in the oven for 10 minutes at 285° F/140° C; then rinse, wash and rinse the cloth in the usual way.

2. With the second method, you must allow the cloth to dry completely, then iron the cloth very thoroughly and evenly for five minutes first on the wrong side and then on the right side of the fabric. In the case of flour-resist, some of the flour paste may begin to crack off at this stage. When the ironing is completed the flour-resist cloth may be immersed in cool water and the flour paste carefully scraped away with a spoon; it may then be washed and ironed in the usual way. Do not allow the flour paste pieces to go down the sink.

7

Design

To make the fullest creative use of an art/craft medium of almost any kind three stages are involved.

In the first stage one must learn the basic principles of the medium (in this case it will be tie and dye, wax batik or flour batik) and some practical knowledge of the materials and dyes used. This first stage is easily attained but even this must involve practical work as well as theoretical reading.

The second stage is to acquire a thorough working knowledge of the principles, based on trial and error and practical experience. There is no substitute for this stage: the insight gained through one's own experience cannot be attained in any other way. The essentials have been described in this book but it is only through practice that you realize the reasons for, and the importance of, the various do's and don'ts. After this time there should be plenty of free experiment. The basic principles must still be adhered to, but other possibilities will begin to occur and you will develop a growing awareness of the potential of the craft.

As you approach the third stage with its limitless possibilities, the practicalities of the craft have been mastered; you have already gone far in discovering your own particular 'bent' or attraction, and an individual style will begin to emerge.

As pointed out in the Introduction, experience in many other fields is not only of use but has great influence on our achievements.

THE USE OF COLOUR IN DESIGN

In designing for utilitarian purposes the choice of colours will be fairly straightforward. Personal taste and the use to which the fabric is to be put will be the main considerations. In the field of creative design for hangings, pictures and decorative fabrics, more understanding and an educated imagination in the use of colour will be called for.

General Principles

Bear in mind the tonal value of the finished work: the most interesting results are likely to be those which have a range of light and dark shades and are not dominated by middle tones. Try to imagine the finished work as it would appear in black and white. If the tones would mostly show as mid-greys then probably some very dark areas, even quite small linear patterns, would add strength and emphasis. Conversely, keep some pale shades but avoid large areas of plain white which can look rather stark. In some cases, of course, one may wish to use white with one plain colour such as navy, for a simple design, for example, for scarves.

Always avoid having equal amounts of colour and tone; instead let one colour predominate and others take a smaller proportion. In actual choice of colour one must bear in mind that dye shades are often put on top of each other thus creating third colours, e.g. white cloth which has been resist-patterned yellow and is resisted again and dyed blue may then become a combination of white, yellow, blue and green. Even these colours may have variations of shade in them according to how they were resisted.

Some recommended colour combinations using only the five Procion colours are: White with lemon yellow, pink, golden yellow, red and red and blue. These colours could give a wide variety of shades ranging from the 'self' colours mentioned and would include shades of orange and red. The red and blue mix of dye would effect a brownish red, on top of yellow colours. White, lemon yellow, pale greenish blue and dark blue make attractive combinations and will produce white, lemon, turquoise, light green and navy.

Golden yellow with either greenish blue or navy will give combinations of yellow and varying shades of green. Very attractive shades of pink, violet, mauve, blackberry and purple may be obtained with red and navy. The rather harsh tone of Red MX 8B may be softened with the addition of only a little of either yellow. Some beautiful rich reds and browns are achieved by varying amounts of red, yellow and blue. As a general rule one finds that lemon yellow MX-6Gs is the colour one uses most of, either as a foundation colour for a design or to add to other colours. The strongest colour of the ones we recommend is the red and it should be used sparingly until one becomes familiar with it.

If one wishes to paint colours directly onto the cloth in the finished shades rather than let the shades build up by successive dyeing, one may mix the dye powders together and then continue as in the recipes. (This method has been used in some of the colour prints of tie and dye.) It is then possible to have colours such as turquoise and mauve or purple on one piece of cloth which otherwise would be difficult to produce by successive dyeings.

THE USE OF SHAPE AND LINE

Have either a predominance of straight lines and angles, with a few curves and circles or the opposite. A design of all curves or all straight lines or an equal amount of each is usually less interesting than a completely balanced pattern. Remember that the spaces left between areas of pattern are just as important as the patterns themselves, so do not attempt to fill the whole cloth with pattern.

In designing a hanging or decorative panel that has a focal point it is usually better to have it rather off centre than for it to be completely symmetrical. In a design which has separate patterns on it, if they are linked together in some way, even by quite simple lines, there will be more sense of impact than when the areas of pattern are left isolated from each other. A border round a piece of work gives it a sense of unity and of being complete in itself. This may also make it seem smaller and slightly more limited. A work without a border and with some shapes or lines appearing only partly on the cloth against the edge, carries the eye outwards, and may make the work seem to be part of a bigger design and in that case bigger in itself. It could also have the effect of making it appear unfinished.

All these considerations must be borne in mind, but once one is aware of them it is not too difficult to decide which kind of design will be best.

INSPIRATION FOR DESIGN

Natural shapes such as seed pods and flower petals; sections through such fruits as tomatoes, pomegranates and peppers; patterns on fishes and birds; colour combinations in flowers; animals, birds and butterflies—all these can give ideas to start a design. In a colour scheme that particularly attracts you, remember that *proportion* of colour is very important, and if this balance is altered it may ruin the effect. Man-made objects may also provide ideas: wrought iron-work, Victorian man-hole covers, piles of land-drain pipes, even industrial objects such as cogs and crank shafts, scaffolding and pylons, can possess interesting shapes and tensions if we are on the lookout for them. Unless one is very skilled at drawing, life-like representations are best avoided, especially any attempt to convey the impression of three dimensions, but this does not mean that animal, bird and fish shapes may not be simplified and stylized.

Museums provide an unlimited source of ideas both in the use of colour and design. Pottery and ceramics are very well worth studying for this reason. Primitive pottery, with its simple, earthy colours, is full of a charm of its own and may teach us much about the use of colour. We need to be constantly 'looking' at the everyday things we see, deciding why we like certain things and what it is that gives them their impact and attraction. This increase of visual awareness will not only help us to develop our own sense of colour and design, but will deepen our appreciation of everything around us.

Suppliers in Great Britain

Procion Dyes 'M' Range
Manutex R.S.
Urea
Resist Salt 'L'
Lissapol

Dylon International Ltd.,
Worsley Bridge Road,
Lower Sydenham,
London SE26 5HD

Acetic Acid
Washing Soda
Beeswax
Candles or Paraffin Wax
Calgon
Bicarbonate of Soda

Boots the Chemist Ltd.,
Also available at most other local Chemists

'Dylon Cold' Dyes

Dylon International Ltd.,
Worsley Bridge Road, Lower Sydenham,
London SE26 5HD

Vinolay Tiles
Craft Knives
Evo-stick

Available at D.I.Y. shops or Ironmongers

Tjanting
Slip trailers
Lino Blocks
Tools
Handles
Flocking Powder
Flocking Mordant

Dryads, Northgates, Leicester

Slip trailer (as illustrated)

Wengers Ltd., Etruria,
Stoke-on-Trent, Staffs

Wooden Shapes for string-block
Hand-made tjap

Made by Dennis Payne, Stockham Way,
Wantage, Berks (*These may be home-made if convenient*)

Suppliers in the USA

Procion Dyes 'M' Range   I.C.I. Organics Inc.,
Resist Salt L   55 Canal Street,
Bicarbonate of Soda   Providence, Rhode Island 02903
Urea
Flocking Powder
Flocking Mordant

Procion Dyes (minimum 1 lb)   Chemical Manufacturing Company,
Lissapol   Madison Avenue, New York, N.Y., 10010

Manutex (Halltex)   Stein Hall & Company Inc.,
    605 Third Avenue, New York, N.Y. 10016

Urea   American Cyanamid Company,
    Dyes Division, Princeton,
    New Jersey 08540

Washing Soda (Salsoda)   Fry Brothers Company,
    104 Blanchard Street, New Jersey

Waxes   Norman Ceramics Co Inc.,
Slip Trailers   252 Mamaroneck Avenue,
    Mamaroneck, New York

Tjanting   Craftool Dyes,
    Wood-Ridge, New Jersey 07075

Lino Blocks   American Crayon Company,
    2002 Hayes Avenue, Sanduskey, Ohio

Tools and Handles   Ontario Knife Company,
    4151, Corbin, Franklinville, New York

Glossary

ACETIC ACID	A non-poisonous, easily obtainable acid to which Procion dye will not reach; it is therefore very useful in ensuring a stronger resist in the dye work.
BATIK	An Indonesian word denoting a resist method of fabric dyeing; usually hot liquid wax, which is painted, drawn or stamped onto the cloth making it resistant to dye in those areas.
BICARBONATE OF SODA (SODIUM BICARBONATE)	An alkali which is used to activate Procion dyes, particularly when used in conjunction with Manutex R.S. thickening. It is also used to neutralize the effect of acetic acid in the process of tie dyeing.
BLOCK PRINTING	A discharge method of printing onto fabric. The block may be made up with string or lino. Potato block printing is not suitable for Procion dyes as the alkalinity in the potato would adversely affect the dye.
CALGON	The trade name for sodium hexametaphosphate—used to soften the water used for dyeing.
DIRECT DYES	'Dylon Cold' is a direct dye which can be used for tie and dye or wax batik work. The manufacturers do not recommend thickening with Manutex. Dylon Cold may be intermixed with the Procion 'M' range of dyes if desired.
EVO-STICK	An impact adhesive used to make string blocks for printing.
FIXING	A process by which the Procion dye is stabilized in its reaction to the cloth. The methods vary in tie and dye and batik, but should be carried out carefully to ensure success.
FLOCK	Fine powdered felt which is used to make a 'pile' on a lino block in order that dye may be absorbed onto the block.
FLOCKING MORDANT	The special adhesive used to stick the powdered flock to the lino block.
FLOUR-RESIST	Sometimes known as starch resist, flour-resist is a method of treating fabric to make it resist the dye in certain areas. Ordinary household flour is mixed with water and applied with a syringe, slip trailer or through a stencil. Thickened dye is brushed over the dry flour paste.
FOUND OBJECTS	Any items such as stones and seeds or cotton reels, cardboard or metal tubes which come to hand and can be used for tying up or for printing work.

Glossary

KELTEX	See Sodium Alginate.
KNOTTING	A technique in tie and dye. The fabric has tied-in knots in pre-determined areas and these areas will not take the dye, so leaving a pattern on the cloth.
LIGHT-FASTNESS	Dyes are said to have certain degrees of light-fastness according to how well they retain their colour on exposure to sunlight or strong daylight. If made up properly, Procion dyes are said by the manufacturers to be 100% fast to sunlight. Many other dyes are not so guaranteed.
LISSAPOL	The brand name for the detergent made by I.C.I. and recommended by them for use in washing off surplus dye from cloth.
MANUTEX	See Sodium Alginate.
PROCION DYES 'M' RANGE	Reactive dyes which link chemically onto the fibres of the cloth. The dyes are then 100% fast to washing and sunlight. Best results are obtained on mercerized cotton or viscose rayon.
RESIST SALT	Used in making up thickening for Procion dyes.
SALSODA	The American equivalent of washing soda.
SODIUM ALGINATE	(Trade name—Manutex, in Britain; Keltex in USA). A thickening agent made from seaweed used with Procion. Its great advantage is that it washes out completely, leaving the fabric soft as new. It is also non-toxic. It is completely stable, and non-variable and non-sticky, and can be thickened to any desired consistency.
TIE AND DYE (TIE DYEING)	A method of resist dyeing. The cloth is tied or bound with string or stones or other objects are tied up in it, and when the cloth is dyed the tied-up areas will have resisted the dye, so leaving a patterned area.
TJAP	'Tjap' is a Malaysian word denoting a metal stamp which is used to apply hot wax to cloth in batik work. The original tjaps were often used to produce highly complicated and delicate designs which also held traditional significance. Simple home-made tjaps may be made even 'found' metal objects may be used to stamp the wax onto the cloth.
UREA (CARBAMIDE)	An ingredient used in making up Procion dye.
TJANTING	A metal tool used in batik work to draw lines or make dots and spots with hot wax on the cloth.
WASHING OFF	A term used to describe the thorough washing and rinsing that is needed to remove surplus dye from the cloth. It is important that washing off should be done very thoroughly in order to obtain clear bright colours.

Books for Further Reading

An Introduction to Textile Printing
    Butterworth in Association with I.C.I. Dyestuffs Division, 3rd Edition, London, 1967.
Tie and Dye as a Present Day Craft by Anne Maile
    Taplinger, New York, 1963; Mills and Boon, London, 1967.
Textile Printing and Dyeing by Nora Proud
    Batsford, London; Reinhold, New York, 1965.
Introducing Batik by Evelyn Samuel
    Batsford, London; Watson-Guptill, New York, 1968.
Batik—Art and Craft by Nik Krevitsky
    Reinhold, New York, 1964.
Batik Fabrics (leaflet) by June Hobson
    Dryad, Leicester.

Weights and Measures

Imperial/US measure	*Approx. Metric equivalent*
1 oz	28·35 gms
1 lb	0·45 kilo
Capacity 1 fluid oz	28·40 ccs
1 imperial pint (20 fluid oz)	568·00 ccs
1 US pint (16 fluid oz)	0·47 litre
1·76 pints	1 litre

Teaspoonful Equivalents of 1 Ounce
The following are only approximate measures, because weights vary according to the sizes of spoons. You can make sure that the same amount is used each time by levelling the powder with a knife.

Substance	British teaspoonfuls	US teaspoonfuls
Manutex powder	10	7½
Resist Salt L powder	4	3
Sodium Bicarbonate powder	6	4½

(4 British teaspoonfuls are the approximate equivalent of 3 US teaspoonfuls)

Temperature
To convert °C into °F, multiply by 9, divide by 5 and add 32.
To convert °F into °C, subtract 32, multiply by 5 and divide by 9.

Index

Acetic acid 26, 67, 75, 77
Adhesives 75, 77
Applying wax 35-6, 41

Batik, wooden frame for 39
Beeswax 36, 42, 75
Bicarbonate of Soda 26, 50, 51, 65, 75, 76
Binding 14-15
Blisters 15
Block printing 77
Brushes 36, 47

Calgon 50, 76
Candles 42, 75
Candle-wax 34, 36
Carbamide 78
Cassava 43
Cellulose fibres 68
Chalk 32
Cold dyes 65, 75
Cold Water dyes 28
Colour combinations 72
'Crackle' effects 36, 41, 47, 50
Craft knives 51, 75

Denman College 7, 11, 45, 59
Direct dyes 28, 77
Direct painting 73
Discharge printing methods 52-63, 77
Disposable syringe 43, 44
Dye fixing 38, 69, 77
Dyeing Flour-Resist Batik 47-48
Dylon Cold dyes 10, 65, 75, 77
Dylon Multipurpose dyes 28

Edge dyeing 26
Equipment 32, 42, 51, 58, 63
Evo-stick 58, 63, 75, 77

Fibres 68
Fixing Procion dye 69, 77
Flocking 61, 62, 75, 77
Flocking mordant 61, 63, 75, 76, 77

Flocking powder 61, 62, 63, 75, 76
Flour paste, resist method 43, 44
Folding and Binding 15-19
Found objects 8, 19, 77

Halltex (Manutex) 76
Handles 75, 76
Hot direct dyes 28

Iron, ironing board 32, 51

Jars 51

Keltex 78
Kitchen mixer 50, 51
Knotting, knots 13, 14, 24

Leaf blocks 53, 56
Light fastness 78
Lino blocks 60-62, 75, 76
Lino cutting handle 63
Lissapol 42, 67, 68, 76, 78

Manutex (Halltex) 7, 45, 48, 50, 62, 63, 75, 78
Marbling 10

Natural fibres 52, 68
Needles 32
Newspaper 42, 51
Nib remover 63

Pad dyeing 52, 55
Paint brushes 36, 42, 51
Painting dye direct onto the fabric 28, 77
Paper template 37
Paraffin wax 42, 75
Parts, folding and dipping 25-26
Pile, on lino block 77
Plastic detergent bottle 43
Plastic bowls, buckets 42
Plastic syringe 43
Plastic foam 52
Plastic washing-up liquid bottle 44
Polythene 26, 38, 51
Pots 51
Printing pad 54, 55, 63
Procion colours 72

Procion dyes 7, 26, 32, 45, 48, 50, 63, 65, 67, 75, 76, 78
Recipes, Dye 67, 68
Removing wax 40
Resist dyeing 77
Resist printing methods 33-51
Resist Salt 'L' 50, 75, 76, 78
Rope method 12
Rubber gloves 42

Salsoda 65, 67, 68, 76, 78
Saucepan 42
Scissors 32
Sewing threads 32
Slip trailer 43, 44, 51, 75, 76, 77
Sodium alginate 78
Sodium bicarbonate 65, 67, 68, 75, 76
Stamps, home-made 42
Starch resist method 77
Stencils 43, 46, 77
Stitching 6, 24, 26
String-block, wooden shapes for 75

Template, paper 37
Thermometer, sugar-boiling 34
Thickening Procion dye 48
Threads, suitable sewing 32
Tjanting 34, 35, 40, 42, 43, 75, 76, 78
Tjap 34, 35, 36, 42, 75, 78
Tools 61, 75, 76
Tritik 7, 22-25
Twisting method 12
Tying up 77

Urea 50, 75, 76, 78
Uses for Tie and Dye 32

Vinolay tiles 43, 46, 51, 75

Washing off 78
Washing soda (Salsoda) 65, 67, 68, 75, 76
Wax applying 35, 40
Waxes 76
Wood, to mount lino 63
Wooden blocks 58